The Constitution of
The State of Florida:
A Quick Reference Guide

Bootblack Budget Books
Copyright 2018 ©
ISBN-13: 978-1985875678
ISBN-10: 1985875675

Contents:

Preamble – Page 21

Article I: Declaration of Rights – Page 22

Section 1. Political Power

Section 2. Basic Rights

Section 3. Religious Freedom

Section 4. Freedom of Speech And Press

Section 5. Right to Assemble

Section 6. Right to Work

Section 7. Military Power

Section 8. Right to Bear Arms

Section 9. Due Process

Section 10. Prohibited Laws

Section 11. Imprisonment for Debt

Section 12. Searches and Seizures

Section 13. Habeas Corpus

Section 14. Pretrial Release and Detention

Section 15. Prosecution for Crime; Offenses Committed by Children

Section 16. Rights of Accused and of Victims

Section 17. Excessive Punishments

Section 18. Administrative Penalties

Section 19. Costs

Section 20. Treason

Section 21. Access to Courts

Section 22. Trial by Jury

Section 23. Right of Privacy

Section 24. Access to Public Records and Meetings

Section 25. Taxpayers Bill of Rights

Section 26. Claimant's Right to Fair Compensation

Section 27. Marriage Defined

Article II: General Provisions – Page 30

Section 1. State Boundaries

Section 2. Seat of Government

Section 3. Branches of Government

Section 4. State Seal and Flag

Section 5. Public Officers

Section 6. Enemy Attack

Section 7. Natural Resources and Scenic Beauty

Section 8. Ethics in Government

Section 9. English is the Official Language of Florida

Article III: Legislature – Page 35

Section 1. Composition

Section 2. Members; Officers

Section 3. Sessions of The Legislature

Section 4. Quorum and Procedure

Section 5. Investigations; Witnesses

Section 6. Laws

Section 7. Passage of Bills

Section 8. Executive Approval and Veto

Section 9. Effective Date of Laws

Section 10. Special Laws

Section 11. Prohibited Special Laws

Section 12. Appropriation Bills

Section 13. Term Of Office

Section 14. Civil Service System

Section 15. Terms and Qualifications of Legislators

Section 16. Legislative Apportionment

Section 17. Impeachment

Section 18. Conflict of Interest

Section 19. State Budgeting, Planning and Appropriations Processes

Section 20. Standards for Establishing Congressional District Boundaries

Section 21. Standards For Establishing Legislative District Boundaries

Article IV: Executive – Page 52

Section 1. Governor

Section 2. Lieutenant Governor

Section 3. Succession to Office of Governor; Acting Governor

Section 4. Cabinet

Section 5. Election of Governor, Lieutenant Governor and Cabinet Members; Qualifications; Terms

Section 6. Executive Departments

Section 7. Suspensions; Filling Office During Suspensions

Section 8. Clemency

Section 9. Fish and Wildlife Conservation Commission

Section 10. Attorney General

Section 11. Department of Veterans Affairs

Section 12. Department of Elderly Affairs

Section 13. Revenue Shortfalls

Article V: Judiciary – Page 60

Section 1. Courts

Section 2. Administration; Practice and Procedure

Section 3. Supreme Court

Section 4. District Courts of Appeal

Section 5. Circuit Courts

Section 6. County Courts

Section 7. Specialized Divisions

Section 8. Eligibility

Section 9. Determination of Number of Judges

Section 10. Retention; Election and Terms

Section 11. Vacancies

Section 12. Discipline; Removal and Retirement

Section 13. Prohibited Activities

Section 14. Funding

Section 15. Attorneys; Admission and Discipline

Section 16. Clerks of The Circuit Courts

Section 17. State Attorneys

Section 18. Public Defenders

Section 19. Judicial Officers as Conservators of The Peace

Section 20. Schedule to Article V

Article VI: Suffrage and Elections – Page 84

Section 1. Regulation of Elections

Section 2. Electors

Section 3. Oath

Section 4. Disqualifications

Section 5. Primary, General, and Special Elections

Section 6. Municipal and District Elections

Section 7. Campaign Spending Limits and Funding of Campaigns for Elective State-Wide Office

Article VII: Finance and Taxation – Page 87

Section 1. Taxation; Appropriations; State Expenses; State Revenue Limitation

Section 2. Taxes; Rate

Section 3. Taxes; Exemptions

Section 4. Taxation; Assessments

Section 5. Estate, Inheritance and Income Taxes

Section 6. Homestead Exemptions

Section 7. Allocation of Pari-Mutuel Taxes

Section 8. Aid to Local Governments

Section 9. Local Taxes

Section 10. Pledging Credit

Section 11. State Bonds; Revenue Bonds

Section 12. Local Bonds

Section 13. Relief From Illegal Taxes

Section 14. Bonds for Pollution Control and Abatement and Other Water Facilities

Section 15. Revenue Bonds for Scholarship Loans

Section 16. Bonds for Housing and Related Facilities

Section 17. Bonds for Acquiring Transportation Right-Of-Way or for Constructing Bridges

Section 18. Laws Requiring Counties or Municipalities to Spend Funds or Limiting Their Ability to Raise Revenue or Receive State Tax Revenue

Article VIII: Local Government – Page 108

Section 1. Counties

Section 2. Municipalities

Section 3. Consolidation.

Section 4. Transfer of Powers

Section 5. Local Option

Section 6. Schedule to Article VIII

Article IX: Education – Page 123

Section 1. Public Education

Section 2. State Board of Education

Section 3. Terms of Appointive Board Members

Section 4. School Districts; School Boards

Section 5. Superintendent of Schools

Section 6. State School Fund

Section 7. State University System

Article X: Miscellaneous – Page 128

Section 1. Amendments to United States Constitution

Section 2. Militia

Section 3. Vacancy in Office

Section 4. Homestead; Exemptions

Section 5. Coverture And Property

Section 6. Eminent Domain

Section 7. Lotteries

Section 8. Census

Section 9. Repeal of Criminal Statutes

Section 10. Felony; Definition

Section 11. Sovereignty Lands

Section 12. Rules of Construction

Section 13. Suits Against the State

Section 14. State Retirement Systems Benefit Changes

Section 15. State Operated Lotteries

Section 16. Limiting Marine Net Fishing

Section 17. Everglades Trust Fund

Section 18. Disposition of Conservation Lands

Section 19. High Speed Ground Transportation System

Section 20. Workplaces Without Tobacco Smoke

Section 21. Limiting Cruel and Inhumane Confinement of Pigs During Pregnancy

Section 22. Parental Notice of Termination of A Minor's Pregnancy

Section 23. Slot Machines

Section 24. Florida Minimum Wage

Section 25. Patients' Right to Know About Adverse Medical Incidents

Section 26. Prohibition of Medical License After Repeated Medical Malpractice

Section 27. Comprehensive Statewide Tobacco Education and Prevention Program

Section 28. Land Acquisition Trust Fund

Section 29. Medical Marijuana Production, Possession and Use

Article XI: Amendments – Page 154

Section 1. Proposal by Legislature

Section 2. Revision Commission

Section 3. Initiative

Section 4. Constitutional Convention

Section 5. Amendment or Revision Election

Section 6. Taxation and Budget Reform Commission

Section 7. Tax or Fee Limitation

Article XII: Schedule – Page 159

Section 1. Constitution of 1885 Superseded

Section 2. Property Taxes; Millages

Section 3. Officers to Continue In Office

Section 4. State Commissioner of Education

Section 5. Superintendent of Schools

Section 6. Laws Preserved

Section 7. Rights Reserved

Section 8. Public Debts Recognized

Section 9. Bonds

Section 10. Preservation of Existing Government

Section 11. Deletion of Obsolete Schedule Items

Section 12. Senators

Section 13. Legislative Apportionment

Section 14. Representatives; Terms

Section 15. Special District Taxes

Section 16. Reorganization

Section 17. Conflicting Provisions

Section 18. Bonds For Housing and Related Facilities

Section 19. Renewable Energy Source Property

Section 20. Access To Public Records

Section 21. State Revenue Limitation

Section 22. Historic Property Exemption and Assessment

Section 23. Fish and Wildlife Conservation Commission

Section 24. Executive Branch Reform

Section 25. Schedule to Article V Amendment

Section 26. Increased Homestead Exemption

Section 27. Property Tax Exemptions and Limitations on Property Tax Assessments

Section 28. Property Tax Exemption and Classification and Assessment of Land Used for Conservation Purposes

Section 29. Limitation on The Assessed Value of Real Property Used for Residential Purposes

Section 30.
   Assessment of Working Waterfront Property

Section 31. Additional Ad Valorem Tax Exemption for Certain Members of The Armed Forces Deployed on Active Duty Outside of The United States

Section 32. Veterans Disabled Due to Combat Injury; Homestead Property Tax Discount

Section 33. Ad Valorem Tax Relief for Surviving Spouses Of Veterans Who Died From Service-Connected Causes and First Responders Who Died in The Line Of Duty

Section 34. Solar Devices or Renewable Energy Source Devices; Exemption From Certain Taxation and Assessment

Section 35. Tax Exemption for Totally and Permanently Disabled First Responders

Section 36. Additional Ad Valorem Exemption for Persons Age Sixty-Five or Older

Preamble:

We, the people of the State of Florida, being grateful to Almighty God for our constitutional liberty, in order to secure its benefits, perfect our government, insure domestic tranquility, maintain public order, and guarantee equal civil and political rights to all, do ordain and establish this constitution.

ARTICLE I: DECLARATION OF RIGHTS

Section 1. Political Power
All political power is inherent in the people. The enunciation herein of certain rights shall not be construed to deny or impair others retained by the people.

Section 2. Basic Rights
All natural persons, female and male alike, are equal before the law and have inalienable rights, among which are the right to enjoy and defend life and liberty, to pursue happiness, to be rewarded for industry, and to acquire, possess and protect property; except that the ownership, inheritance, disposition and possession of real property by aliens ineligible for citizenship may be regulated or prohibited by law. No person shall be deprived of any right because of race, religion, national origin, or physical disability.

Section 3. Religious Freedom
There shall be no law respecting the establishment of religion or prohibiting or penalizing the free exercise thereof. Religious freedom shall not justify practices inconsistent with public morals, peace or safety. No revenue of the state or any political subdivision or agency thereof shall ever be taken from the public treasury directly or indirectly in aid of any church, sect, or religious denomination or in aid of any sectarian institution.

Section 4. Freedom of Speech and Press
Every person may speak, write and publish sentiments on all subjects but shall be responsible for the abuse of that right. No law shall be passed to restrain or abridge the liberty of speech or of the press. In all criminal prosecutions and civil actions for defamation the truth may be given in evidence. If the matter charged as defamatory is true and was published with good motives, the party shall be acquitted or exonerated.

Section 5. Right to Assemble
The people shall have the right peaceably to assemble, to instruct their representatives, and to petition for redress of grievances.

Section 6. Right to Work
The right of persons to work shall not be denied or abridged on account of membership or non-membership in any labor union or labor organization. The right of employees, by and through a labor organization, to bargain collectively shall not be denied or abridged. Public employees shall not have the right to strike.

Section 7. Military Power
The military power shall be subordinate to the civil.

Section 8. Right to Bear Arms

(a) The right of the people to keep and bear arms in defense of themselves and of the lawful authority of the state shall not be infringed, except that the manner of bearing arms may be regulated by law.
(b) There shall be a mandatory period of three days, excluding weekends and legal holidays, between the purchase and delivery at retail of any handgun. For the purposes of this section, "purchase" means the transfer of money or other valuable consideration to the retailer, and "handgun" means a firearm capable of being carried and used by one hand, such as a pistol or revolver. Holders of a concealed weapon permit as prescribed in Florida law shall not be subject to the provisions of this paragraph.
(c) The legislature shall enact legislation implementing subsection (b) of this section, effective no later than December 31, 1991, which shall provide that anyone violating the provisions of subsection (b) shall be guilty of a felony.
(d) This restriction shall not apply to a trade in of another handgun.

Section 9. Due Process
No person shall be deprived of life, liberty or property without due process of law, or be twice put in jeopardy for the same offense, or be compelled in any criminal matter to be a witness against oneself.

Section 10. Prohibited Laws
No bill of attainder, ex post facto law or law impairing the obligation of contracts shall be passed.

Section 11. Imprisonment for Debt
No person shall be imprisoned for debt, except in cases of fraud.

Section 12. Searches and Seizures
The right of the people to be secure in their persons, houses, papers and effects against unreasonable searches and seizures, and against the unreasonable interception of private communications by any means, shall not be violated. No warrant shall be issued except upon probable cause, supported by affidavit, particularly describing the place or places to be searched, the person or persons, thing or things to be seized, the communication to be intercepted, and the nature of evidence to be obtained. This right shall be construed in conformity with the 4th Amendment to the United States Constitution, as interpreted by the United States Supreme Court. Articles or information obtained in violation of this right shall not be admissible in evidence if such articles or information would be inadmissible under decisions of the United States Supreme Court construing the 4th Amendment to the United States Constitution.

Section 13. Habeas Corpus
The writ of habeas corpus shall be grantable of right, freely and without cost. It shall be returnable without delay, and shall never be suspended unless, in case of rebellion or invasion, suspension is essential to the public safety.

Section 14. Pretrial Release and Detention
Unless charged with a capital offense or an offense punishable by life imprisonment and the proof of guilt is evident or the presumption is great, every person charged with a crime or violation of municipal or county ordinance shall be entitled to pretrial release on reasonable conditions. If no conditions of release can reasonably protect the community from risk of physical harm to persons, assure the presence of the accused at trial, or assure the integrity of the judicial process, the accused may be detained.

Section 15. Prosecution for Crime; Offenses Committed by Children

(a) No person shall be tried for capital crime without presentment or indictment by a grand jury, or for other felony without such presentment or indictment or an information under oath filed by the prosecuting officer of the court, except persons on active duty in the militia when tried by courts martial.
(b) When authorized by law, a child as therein defined may be charged with a violation of law as an act of delinquency instead of crime and tried without a jury or other requirements applicable to criminal cases. Any child so charged shall, upon demand made as provided by law before a trial in a juvenile proceeding, be tried in an appropriate court as an adult. A child found delinquent shall be disciplined as provided by law.

Section 16. Rights of Accused and of Victims

(a) In all criminal prosecutions the accused shall, upon demand, be informed of the nature and cause of the accusation, and shall be furnished a copy of the charges, and shall have the right to have compulsory process for witnesses, to confront at trial adverse witnesses, to be heard in person, by counsel or both, and to have a speedy and public trial by impartial jury in the county where the crime was committed. If the county is not known, the indictment or information may charge venue in two or more counties conjunctively and proof that the crime was

committed in that area shall be sufficient; but before pleading the accused may elect in which of those counties the trial will take place. Venue for prosecution of crimes committed beyond the boundaries of the state shall be fixed by law.
(b) Victims of crime or their lawful representatives, including the next of kin of homicide victims, are entitled to the right to be informed, to be present, and to be heard when relevant, at all crucial stages of criminal proceedings, to the extent that these rights do not interfere with the constitutional rights of the accused.

Section 17. Excessive Punishments
Excessive fines, cruel and unusual punishment, attainder, forfeiture of estate, indefinite imprisonment, and unreasonable detention of witnesses are forbidden. The death penalty is an authorized punishment for capital crimes designated by the legislature. The prohibition against cruel or unusual punishment, and the prohibition against cruel and unusual punishment, shall be construed in conformity with decisions of the United States Supreme Court which interpret the prohibition against cruel and unusual punishment provided in the Eighth Amendment to the United States Constitution. Any method of execution shall be allowed, unless prohibited by the United States Constitution. Methods of execution may be designated by the legislature, and a change in any method of execution may be applied retroactively. A sentence of death shall not be reduced on the basis that a method of execution is invalid. In any case in which an execution method is declared invalid, the death sentence shall remain in force until the sentence can be lawfully executed by any valid method. This section shall apply retroactively.

Section 18. Administrative Penalties
No administrative agency, except the Department of Military Affairs in an appropriately convened court-martial action as provided by law, shall impose a sentence of imprisonment, nor shall it impose any other penalty except as provided by law.

Section 19. Costs
No person charged with crime shall be compelled to pay costs before a judgment of conviction has become final.

Section 20. Treason
Treason against the state shall consist only in levying war against it, adhering to its enemies, or giving them aid and comfort, and no person shall be convicted of treason except on the testimony of two witnesses to the same overt act or on confession in open court.

Section 21. Access to Courts
The courts shall be open to every person for redress of any injury, and justice shall be administered without sale, denial or delay.

Section 22. Trial by Jury
The right of trial by jury shall be secure to all and remain inviolate. The qualifications and the number of jurors, not fewer than six, shall be fixed by law.

Section 23. Right of Privacy
Every natural person has the right to be let alone and free from governmental intrusion into the person's private life except as otherwise provided herein. This section shall not be construed to limit the public's right of access to public records and meetings as provided by law.

Section 24. Access to Public Records and Meetings

(a) Every person has the right to inspect or copy any public record made or received in connection with the official business of any public body, officer, or employee of the state, or persons acting on their behalf, except with respect to records exempted pursuant to this section or specifically made confidential by this Constitution. This section specifically includes the legislative, executive, and judicial branches of government and each agency or department created thereunder; counties, municipalities, and districts; and each constitutional officer, board, and commission, or entity created pursuant to law or this Constitution.

(b) All meetings of any collegial public body of the executive branch of state government or of any collegial public body of a county, municipality, school district, or special district, at which official acts are to be taken or at which public business of such body is to be transacted or discussed, shall be open and noticed to the public and meetings of the legislature shall be open and noticed as provided in Article III, Section 4(e), except with respect to meetings exempted pursuant to this section or specifically closed by this Constitution.

(c) This section shall be self-executing. The legislature, however, may provide by general law passed by a two-thirds vote of each house for the exemption of records from the requirements of subsection (a) and the exemption of meetings from the requirements of subsection (b), provided that such law shall state with specificity the public necessity justifying the exemption and shall be no broader than necessary to accomplish the stated purpose of the law. The legislature shall enact laws governing the enforcement of this section, including the maintenance, control, destruction, disposal, and disposition of records made public by this section, except that each house of the legislature may adopt rules governing the enforcement of this section in relation to records of the legislative branch. Laws enacted pursuant to this subsection shall contain only exemptions from the requirements of subsections (a) or (b) and provisions governing the enforcement of this section, and shall relate to one subject.

(d) All laws that are in effect on July 1, 1993 that limit public access to records or meetings shall remain in force, and such laws apply to records of the legislative and judicial branches, until they are repealed. Rules of court that are in effect on the date of adoption of this section that limit access to records shall remain in effect until they are repealed.

Section 25. Taxpayers' Bill of Rights
By general law the legislature shall prescribe and adopt a Taxpayers' Bill of Rights that, in clear and concise language, sets forth taxpayers' rights and responsibilities and government's responsibilities to deal fairly with taxpayers under the laws of this state. This section shall be effective July 1, 1993.

Section 26. Claimant's Right to Fair Compensation

(a) Article I, Section 26 is created to read "Claimant's right to fair compensation." In any medical liability claim involving a contingency fee, the claimant is entitled to receive no less than 70% of the first $250,000.00 in all damages received by the claimant, exclusive of reasonable and customary costs, whether received by judgment, settlement, or otherwise, and regardless of the number of defendants. The claimant is entitled to 90% of all damages in excess of $250,000.00, exclusive of reasonable and customary costs and regardless of the number of defendants. This provision is self-executing and does not require implementing legislation.
(b) This Amendment shall take effect on the day following approval by the voters.

Section 27. Marriage Defined
Inasmuch as marriage is the legal union of only one man and one woman as husband and wife, no other legal union that is treated as marriage or the substantial equivalent thereof shall be valid or recognized.

ARTICLE II: GENERAL PROVISIONS

Section 1. State Boundaries

(a) The state boundaries are: Begin at the mouth of the Perdido River, which for the purposes of this description is defined as the point where latitude 30°16'53" north and longitude 87°31'06" west intersect; thence to the point where latitude 30°17'02" north and longitude 87°31'06" west intersect; thence to the point where latitude 30°18'00" north and longitude 87°27'08" west intersect; thence to the point where the center line of the Intracoastal Canal (as the same existed on June 12, 1953) and longitude 87°27'00" west intersect; the same being in the middle of the Perdido River; thence up the middle of the Perdido River to the point where it intersects the south boundary of the State of Alabama, being also the point of intersection of the middle of the Perdido River with latitude 31°00'00" north; thence east, along the south boundary line of the State of Alabama, the same being latitude 31°00'00" north to the middle of the Chattahoochee River; thence down the middle of said river to its confluence with the Flint River; thence in a straight line to the head of the St. Marys River; thence down the middle of said river to the Atlantic Ocean; thence due east to the edge of the Gulf Stream or a distance of three geographic miles whichever is the greater distance; thence in a southerly direction along the edge of the Gulf Stream or along a line three geographic miles from the Atlantic coastline and three leagues distant from the Gulf of Mexico coastline, whichever is greater, to and through the Straits of Florida and westerly, including the Florida reefs, to a point due south of and three leagues from the southernmost point of the Marquesas Keys; thence westerly along a straight line to a point due south of and three leagues from Loggerhead Key, the westernmost of the Dry Tortugas Islands; thence westerly, northerly and easterly along the arc of a curve three leagues distant from Loggerhead Key to a point due north of Loggerhead Key; thence northeast along a straight line to a point three leagues from the coastline of Florida; thence northerly and westerly three leagues distant from the coastline to a point west

of the mouth of the Perdido River three leagues from the coastline as measured on a line bearing south 0°01'00" west from the point of beginning; thence northerly along said line to the point of beginning. The State of Florida shall also include any additional territory within the United States adjacent to the Peninsula of Florida lying south of the St. Marys River, east of the Perdido River, and south of the States of Alabama and Georgia.
(b) The coastal boundaries may be extended by statute to the limits permitted by the laws of the United States or international law.

Section 2. Seat of Government
The seat of government shall be the City of Tallahassee, in Leon County, where the offices of the governor, lieutenant governor, cabinet members and the supreme court shall be maintained and the sessions of the legislature shall be held; provided that, in time of invasion or grave emergency, the governor by proclamation may for the period of the emergency transfer the seat of government to another place.

Section 3. Branches of Government
The powers of the state government shall be divided into legislative, executive and judicial branches. No person belonging to one branch shall exercise any powers appertaining to either of the other branches unless expressly provided herein.

Section 4. State Seal and Flag
The design of the great seal and flag of the state shall be prescribed by law.

Section 5. Public Officers

(a) No person holding any office of emolument under any foreign government, or civil office of emolument under the United States or any other state, shall hold any office of honor or of emolument under the government of this state. No person shall hold at the same time more than one office under the government of the state and the counties and municipalities therein, except that a notary public or military officer may hold another office, and any officer may be a member of a constitution revision commission, taxation and budget reform commission, constitutional convention, or statutory body having only advisory powers.

(b) Each state and county officer, before entering upon the duties of the office, shall give bond as required by law, and shall swear or affirm:

"I do solemnly swear (or affirm) that I will support, protect, and defend the Constitution and Government of the United States and of the State of Florida; that I am duly qualified to hold office under the Constitution of the state; and that I will well and faithfully perform the duties of   (title of office)   on which I am now about to enter. So help me God.",

and thereafter shall devote personal attention to the duties of the office, and continue in office until a successor qualifies.

(c) The powers, duties, compensation and method of payment of state and county officers shall be fixed by law.

Section 6. Enemy Attack

In periods of emergency resulting from enemy attack the legislature shall have power to provide for prompt and temporary succession to the powers and duties of all public offices the incumbents of which may become unavailable to execute the functions of their offices, and to adopt such other measures as may be necessary and appropriate to insure the continuity of governmental operations during the emergency. In exercising these powers, the legislature may depart from other requirements of this constitution, but only to the extent necessary to meet the emergency.

Section 7. Natural Resources and Scenic Beauty

(a) It shall be the policy of the state to conserve and protect its natural resources and scenic beauty. Adequate provision shall be made by law for the abatement of air and water pollution and of excessive and unnecessary noise and for the conservation and protection of natural resources.

(b) Those in the Everglades Agricultural Area who cause water pollution within the Everglades Protection Area or the Everglades Agricultural Area shall be primarily responsible for paying the costs of the abatement of that pollution. For the purposes of this subsection, the terms "Everglades Protection Area" and "Everglades Agricultural Area" shall have the meanings as defined in statutes in effect on January 1, 1996.

Section 8. Ethics in Government
A public office is a public trust. The people shall have the right to secure and sustain that trust against abuse. To assure this right:

(a) All elected constitutional officers and candidates for such offices and, as may be determined by law, other public officers, candidates, and employees shall file full and public disclosure of their financial interests.
(b) All elected public officers and candidates for such offices shall file full and public disclosure of their campaign finances.
(c) Any public officer or employee who breaches the public trust for private gain and any person or entity inducing such breach shall be liable to the state for all financial benefits obtained by such actions. The manner of recovery and additional damages may be provided by law.
(d) Any public officer or employee who is convicted of a felony involving a breach of public trust shall be subject to forfeiture of rights and privileges under a public retirement system or pension plan in such manner as may be provided by law.
(e) No member of the legislature or statewide elected officer shall personally represent another person or entity for compensation before the government body or agency of which the individual was an officer or member for a period of two years following vacation of office. No member of the legislature shall personally represent another person or entity for compensation during term of office before any state agency other than judicial tribunals. Similar restrictions on other public officers and employees may be established by law.
(f) There shall be an independent commission to conduct investigations and make public reports on all complaints

concerning breach of public trust by public officers or employees not within the jurisdiction of the judicial qualifications commission.

(g) A code of ethics for all state employees and nonjudicial officers prohibiting conflict between public duty and private interests shall be prescribed by law.

(h) This section shall not be construed to limit disclosures and prohibitions which may be established by law to preserve the public trust and avoid conflicts between public duties and private interests.

(i) Schedule—On the effective date of this amendment and until changed by law:

(1) Full and public disclosure of financial interests shall mean filing with the custodian of state records by July 1 of each year a sworn statement showing net worth and identifying each asset and liability in excess of $1,000 and its value together with one of the following:

a. A copy of the person's most recent federal income tax return; or

b. A sworn statement which identifies each separate source and amount of income which exceeds $1,000. The forms for such source disclosure and the rules under which they are to be filed shall be prescribed by the independent commission established in subsection (f), and such rules shall include disclosure of secondary sources of income.

(2) Persons holding statewide elective offices shall also file disclosure of their financial interests pursuant to subsection (i)(1).

(3) The independent commission provided for in subsection (f) shall mean the Florida Commission on Ethics.

Section 9. English is the Official Language of Florida

(a) English is the official language of the State of Florida.

(b) The legislature shall have the power to enforce this section by appropriate legislation.

ARTICLE III: LEGISLATURE

Section 1. Composition The legislative power of the state shall be vested in a legislature of the State of Florida, consisting of a senate composed of one senator elected from each senatorial district and a house of representatives composed of one member elected from each representative district.

Section 2. Members; Officers
Each house shall be the sole judge of the qualifications, elections, and returns of its members, and shall biennially choose its officers, including a permanent presiding officer selected from its membership, who shall be designated in the senate as President of the Senate, and in the house as Speaker of the House of Representatives. The senate shall designate a Secretary to serve at its pleasure, and the house of representatives shall designate a Clerk to serve at its pleasure. The legislature shall appoint an auditor to serve at its pleasure who shall audit public records and perform related duties as prescribed by law or concurrent resolution.

Section 3. Sessions of the Legislature

(a) ORGANIZATION SESSIONS. On the fourteenth day following each general election the legislature shall convene for the exclusive purpose of organization and selection of officers.
(b) REGULAR SESSIONS. A regular session of the legislature shall convene on the first Tuesday after the first Monday in March of each odd-numbered year, and on the first Tuesday after the first Monday in March, or such other date as may be fixed by law, of each even-numbered year.
(c) SPECIAL SESSIONS.

(1) The governor, by proclamation stating the purpose, may convene the legislature in special session during which only such legislative business may be transacted as is within the purview of the proclamation, or of a communication from the governor, or is introduced by consent of two-thirds of the membership of each

house.
(2) A special session of the legislature may be convened as provided by law.

(d) LENGTH OF SESSIONS. A regular session of the legislature shall not exceed sixty consecutive days, and a special session shall not exceed twenty consecutive days, unless extended beyond such limit by a three-fifths vote of each house. During such an extension no new business may be taken up in either house without the consent of two-thirds of its membership.
(e) ADJOURNMENT. Neither house shall adjourn for more than seventy-two consecutive hours except pursuant to concurrent resolution.
(f) ADJOURNMENT BY GOVERNOR. If, during any regular or special session, the two houses cannot agree upon a time for adjournment, the governor may adjourn the session sine die or to any date within the period authorized for such session; provided that, at least twenty-four hours before adjourning the session, and while neither house is in recess, each house shall be given formal written notice of the governor's intention to do so, and agreement reached within that period by both houses on a time for adjournment shall prevail.

Section 4. Quorum and Procedure

(a) A majority of the membership of each house shall constitute a quorum, but a smaller number may adjourn from day to day and compel the presence of absent members in such manner and under such penalties as it may prescribe. Each house shall determine its rules of procedure.
(b) Sessions of each house shall be public; except sessions of the senate when considering appointment to or removal from public office may be closed.
(c) Each house shall keep and publish a journal of its proceedings; and upon the request of five members present, the vote of each member voting on any question shall be entered on the journal. In any legislative committee or subcommittee, the vote of each member voting on the final passage of any

legislation pending before the committee, and upon the request of any two members of the committee or subcommittee, the vote of each member on any other question, shall be recorded.

(d) Each house may punish a member for contempt or disorderly conduct and, by a two-thirds vote of its membership, may expel a member.

(e) The rules of procedure of each house shall provide that all legislative committee and subcommittee meetings of each house, and joint conference committee meetings, shall be open and noticed to the public. The rules of procedure of each house shall further provide that all prearranged gatherings, between more than two members of the legislature, or between the governor, the president of the senate, or the speaker of the house of representatives, the purpose of which is to agree upon formal legislative action that will be taken at a subsequent time, or at which formal legislative action is taken, regarding pending legislation or amendments, shall be reasonably open to the public. All open meetings shall be subject to order and decorum. This section shall be implemented and defined by the rules of each house, and such rules shall control admission to the floor of each legislative chamber and may, where reasonably necessary for security purposes or to protect a witness appearing before a committee, provide for the closure of committee meetings. Each house shall be the sole judge for the interpretation, implementation, and enforcement of this section.

Section 5. Investigations; Witnesses

Each house, when in session, may compel attendance of witnesses and production of documents and other evidence upon any matter under investigation before it or any of its committees, and may punish by fine not exceeding one thousand dollars or imprisonment not exceeding ninety days, or both, any person not a member who has been guilty of disorderly or contemptuous conduct in its presence or has refused to obey its lawful summons or to answer lawful questions. Such powers, except the power to punish, may be conferred by law upon committees when the legislature is not in session. Punishment of contempt of an interim legislative committee shall be by judicial proceedings as prescribed by law.

Section 6. Laws
Every law shall embrace but one subject and matter properly connected therewith, and the subject shall be briefly expressed in the title. No law shall be revised or amended by reference to its title only. Laws to revise or amend shall set out in full the revised or amended act, section, subsection or paragraph of a subsection. The enacting clause of every law shall read: "Be It Enacted by the Legislature of the State of Florida:".

Section 7. Passage Of Bills
Any bill may originate in either house and after passage in one may be amended in the other. It shall be read in each house on three separate days, unless this rule is waived by two-thirds vote; provided the publication of its title in the journal of a house shall satisfy the requirement for the first reading in that house. On each reading, it shall be read by title only, unless one-third of the members present desire it read in full. On final passage, the vote of each member voting shall be entered on the journal. Passage of a bill shall require a majority vote in each house. Each bill and joint resolution passed in both houses shall be signed by the presiding officers of the respective houses and by the secretary of the senate and the clerk of the house of representatives during the session or as soon as practicable after its adjournment sine die.

Section 8. Executive Approval and Veto

(a) Every bill passed by the legislature shall be presented to the governor for approval and shall become a law if the governor approves and signs it, or fails to veto it within seven consecutive days after presentation. If during that period or on the seventh day the legislature adjourns sine die or takes a recess of more than thirty days, the governor shall have fifteen consecutive days from the date of presentation to act on the bill. In all cases except general appropriation bills, the veto shall extend to the entire bill. The governor may veto any specific appropriation in a general appropriation bill, but may not veto any qualification or restriction without also vetoing the appropriation to which it relates.

(b) When a bill or any specific appropriation of a general appropriation bill has been vetoed, the governor shall transmit signed objections thereto to the house in which the bill originated if in session. If that house is not in session, the governor shall file them with the custodian of state records, who shall lay them before that house at its next regular or special session, whichever occurs first, and they shall be entered on its journal. If the originating house votes to re-enact a vetoed measure, whether in a regular or special session, and the other house does not consider or fails to re-enact the vetoed measure, no further consideration by either house at any subsequent session may be taken. If a vetoed measure is presented at a special session and the originating house does not consider it, the measure will be available for consideration at any intervening special session and until the end of the next regular session.

(c) If each house shall, by a two-thirds vote, re-enact the bill or reinstate the vetoed specific appropriation of a general appropriation bill, the vote of each member voting shall be entered on the respective journals, and the bill shall become law or the specific appropriation reinstated, the veto notwithstanding.

Section 9. Effective Date of Laws

Each law shall take effect on the sixtieth day after adjournment sine die of the session of the legislature in which enacted or as otherwise provided therein. If the law is passed over the veto of the governor it shall take effect on the sixtieth day after adjournment sine die of the session in which the veto is overridden, on a later date fixed in the law, or on a date fixed by resolution passed by both houses of the legislature.

Section 10. Special Laws

No special law shall be passed unless notice of intention to seek enactment thereof has been published in the manner provided by general law. Such notice shall not be necessary when the law, except the provision for referendum, is conditioned to become effective only upon approval by vote of the electors of the area affected.

Section 11. Prohibited Special Laws

(a) There shall be no special law or general law of local application pertaining to:

(1) election, jurisdiction or duties of officers, except officers of municipalities, chartered counties, special districts or local governmental agencies;
(2) assessment or collection of taxes for state or county purposes, including extension of time therefor, relief of tax officers from due performance of their duties, and relief of their sureties from liability;
(3) rules of evidence in any court;
(4) punishment for crime;
(5) petit juries, including compensation of jurors, except establishment of jury commissions;
(6) change of civil or criminal venue;
(7) conditions precedent to bringing any civil or criminal proceedings, or limitations of time therefor;
(8) refund of money legally paid or remission of fines, penalties or forfeitures;
(9) creation, enforcement, extension or impairment of liens based on private contracts, or fixing of interest rates on private contracts;
(10) disposal of public property, including any interest therein, for private purposes;
(11) vacation of roads;
(12) private incorporation or grant of privilege to a private corporation;
(13) effectuation of invalid deeds, wills or other instruments, or

change in the law of descent;
(14) change of name of any person;
(15) divorce;
(16) legitimation or adoption of persons;
(17) relief of minors from legal disabilities;
(18) transfer of any property interest of persons under legal disabilities or of estates of decedents;
(19) hunting or fresh water fishing;
(20) regulation of occupations which are regulated by a state agency; or
(21) any subject when prohibited by general law passed by a three-fifths vote of the membership of each house. Such law may be amended or repealed by like vote.

(b) In the enactment of general laws on other subjects, political subdivisions or other governmental entities may be classified only on a basis reasonably related to the subject of the law.

Section 12. Appropriation Bills
Laws making appropriations for salaries of public officers and other current expenses of the state shall contain provisions on no other subject.

Section 13. Term of Office
No office shall be created the term of which shall exceed four years except as provided herein.

Section 14. Civil Service System
By law there shall be created a civil service system for state employees, except those expressly exempted, and there may be created civil service systems and boards for county, district or municipal employees and for such offices thereof as are not elected or appointed by the governor, and there may be authorized such boards as are necessary to prescribe the qualifications, method of selection and tenure of such employees and officers.

Section 15. Terms and Qualifications of Legislators

(a) Senators. Senators shall be elected for terms of four years, those from odd-numbered districts in the years the numbers of which are multiples of four and those from even-numbered districts in even-numbered years the numbers of which are not multiples of four; except, at the election next following a reapportionment, some senators shall be elected for terms of two years when necessary to maintain staggered terms.
(b) Representatives. Members of the house of representatives shall be elected for terms of two years in each even-numbered year.
(c) Qualifications. Each legislator shall be at least twenty-one years of age, an elector and resident of the district from which elected and shall have resided in the state for a period of two years prior to election.
(d) Assuming Office; Vacancies. Members of the legislature shall take office upon election. Vacancies in legislative office shall be filled only by election as provided by law.

Section 16. Legislative Apportionment

(a) Senatorial and Representative Districts. The legislature at its regular session in the second year following each decennial census, by joint resolution, shall apportion the state in accordance with the constitution of the state and of the United States into not less than thirty nor more than forty consecutively numbered senatorial districts of either contiguous, overlapping or identical territory, and into not less than eighty nor more than one hundred twenty consecutively numbered representative districts of either contiguous, overlapping or identical territory. Should that session adjourn without adopting such joint resolution, the governor by proclamation shall reconvene the legislature within thirty days in special apportionment session which shall not exceed thirty consecutive days, during which no other business shall be transacted, and it shall be the mandatory duty of the legislature to adopt a joint resolution of apportionment.

(b) Failure of Legislature to Apportion; Judicial Reapportionment. In the event a special apportionment session of the legislature finally adjourns without adopting a joint resolution of apportionment, the attorney general shall, within five days, petition the supreme court of the state to make such apportionment. No later than the sixtieth day after the filing of such petition, the supreme court shall file with the custodian of state records an order making such apportionment.

(c) Judicial Review of Apportionment. Within fifteen days after the passage of the joint resolution of apportionment, the attorney general shall petition the supreme court of the state for a declaratory judgment determining the validity of the apportionment. The supreme court, in accordance with its rules, shall permit adversary interests to present their views and, within thirty days from the filing of the petition, shall enter its judgment.

(d) Effect of Judgment in Apportionment; Extraordinary Apportionment Session. A judgment of the supreme court of the state determining the apportionment to be valid shall be binding upon all the citizens of the state. Should the supreme court determine that the apportionment made by the legislature is invalid, the governor by proclamation shall reconvene the legislature within five days thereafter in extraordinary apportionment session which shall not exceed fifteen days, during which the legislature shall adopt a joint resolution of apportionment conforming to the judgment of the supreme court.

(e) Extraordinary Apportionment Session; Review of Apportionment. Within fifteen days after the adjournment of an extraordinary apportionment session, the attorney general shall file a petition in the supreme court of the state setting forth the apportionment resolution adopted by the legislature, or if none has been adopted reporting that fact to the court. Consideration of the validity of a joint resolution of apportionment shall be had as provided for in cases of such joint resolution adopted at a regular or special apportionment session.

(f) Judicial Reapportionment. Should an extraordinary apportionment session fail to adopt a resolution of apportionment or should the supreme court determine that the apportionment made is invalid, the court shall, not later than sixty days after receiving the petition of the attorney general, file with the custodian of state records an order making such apportionment.

Section 17. Impeachment

(a) The governor, lieutenant governor, members of the cabinet, justices of the supreme court, judges of district courts of appeal, judges of circuit courts, and judges of county courts shall be liable to impeachment for misdemeanor in office. The house of representatives by two-thirds vote shall have the power to impeach an officer. The speaker of the house of representatives shall have power at any time to appoint a committee to investigate charges against any officer subject to impeachment.
(b) An officer impeached by the house of representatives shall be disqualified from performing any official duties until acquitted by the senate, and, unless impeached, the governor may by appointment fill the office until completion of the trial.
(c) All impeachments by the house of representatives shall be tried by the senate. The chief justice of the supreme court, or another justice designated by the chief justice, shall preside at the trial, except in a trial of the chief justice, in which case the governor shall preside. The senate shall determine the time for the trial of any impeachment and may sit for the trial whether the house of representatives be in session or not. The time fixed for trial shall not be more than six months after the impeachment. During an impeachment trial senators shall be upon their oath or affirmation. No officer shall be convicted without the concurrence of two-thirds of the members of the senate present. Judgment of conviction in cases of impeachment shall remove the offender from office and, in the discretion of the senate, may include disqualification to hold any office of honor, trust or profit. Conviction or acquittal shall not affect the civil or criminal responsibility of the officer.

Section 18. Conflict of Interest
A code of ethics for all state employees and nonjudicial officers prohibiting conflict between public duty and private interests shall be prescribed by law.

Section 19. State Budgeting, Planning and Appropriations Processes

(a) Annual Budgeting

(1) General law shall prescribe the adoption of annual state budgetary and planning processes and require that detail reflecting the annualized costs of the state budget and reflecting the nonrecurring costs of the budget requests shall accompany state department and agency legislative budget requests, the governor's recommended budget, and appropriation bills.
(2) Unless approved by a three-fifths vote of the membership of each house, appropriations made for recurring purposes from nonrecurring general revenue funds for any fiscal year shall not exceed three percent of the total general revenue funds estimated to be available at the time such appropriation is made.
(3) As prescribed by general law, each state department and agency shall be required to submit a legislative budget request that is based upon and that reflects the long-range financial outlook adopted by the joint legislative budget commission or that specifically explains any variance from the long-range financial outlook contained in the request.
(4) For purposes of this section, the terms department and agency shall include the judicial branch.

(b) Appropriation Bills Format. Separate sections within the general appropriation bill shall be used for each major program area of the state budget; major program areas shall include: education enhancement "lottery" trust fund items; education (all other funds); human services; criminal justice and corrections; natural resources, environment, growth management, and transportation; general government; and judicial branch. Each major program area shall include an itemization of expenditures for: state operations; state capital outlay; aid to local governments and nonprofit organizations operations; aid to local governments and nonprofit organizations capital outlay; federal funds and the associated state matching funds; spending authorizations for operations; and spending authorizations for capital outlay. Additionally, appropriation bills passed by the legislature shall include an itemization of specific appropriations that exceed one million dollars ($1,000,000.00) in 1992 dollars. For purposes of this subsection, "specific appropriation," "itemization," and "major program area" shall be defined by law. This itemization threshold shall be adjusted by general law every four years to reflect the rate of inflation or deflation as indicated in the Consumer Price Index for All Urban Consumers, U.S. City Average, All Items, or successor reports as reported by the United States Department of Labor, Bureau of Labor Statistics or its successor. Substantive bills containing appropriations shall also be subject to the itemization requirement mandated under this provision and shall be subject to the governor's specific appropriation veto power described in Article III, Section 8.

(c) Appropriations Process.

(1) No later than September 15 of each year, the joint legislative budget commission shall issue a long-range financial outlook setting out recommended fiscal strategies for the state and its departments and agencies in order to assist the legislature in making budget decisions. The long-range financial outlook must include major workload and revenue estimates. In order to implement this paragraph, the joint legislative budget commission shall use current official consensus estimates and may request the development of additional official estimates.
(2) The joint legislative budget commission shall seek input from the public and from the executive and judicial branches when developing and recommending the long-range financial outlook.
(3) The legislature shall prescribe by general law conditions under which limited adjustments to the budget, as recommended by the governor or the chief justice of the supreme court, may be approved without the concurrence of the full legislature.

(d) Seventy-Two Hour Public Review Period. All general appropriation bills shall be furnished to each member of the legislature, each member of the cabinet, the governor, and the chief justice of the supreme court at least seventy-two hours before final passage by either house of the legislature of the bill in the form that will be presented to the governor.
(e) Final Budget Report. A final budget report shall be prepared as prescribed by general law. The final budget report shall be produced no later than the 120th day after the beginning of the fiscal year, and copies of the report shall be furnished to each member of the legislature, the head of each department and agency of the state, the auditor general, and the chief justice of the supreme court.
(f) Trust Funds.

(1) No trust fund of the State of Florida or other public body may be created or re-created by law without a three-fifths vote of the membership of each house of the legislature in a separate bill for that purpose only.
(2) State trust funds shall terminate not more than four years after the effective date of the act authorizing the initial creation of the trust fund. By law the legislature may set a shorter time period for which any trust fund is authorized.
(3) Trust funds required by federal programs or mandates; trust funds established for bond covenants, indentures, or resolutions, whose revenues are legally pledged by the state or public body to meet debt service or other financial requirements of any debt obligations of the state or any public body; the state transportation trust fund; the trust fund containing the net annual proceeds from the Florida Education Lotteries; the Florida retirement trust fund; trust funds for institutions under the management of the Board of Governors, where such trust funds are for auxiliary enterprises and contracts, grants, and donations, as those terms are defined by general law; trust funds that serve as clearing funds or accounts for the chief financial officer or state agencies; trust funds that account for assets held by the state in a trustee capacity as an agent or fiduciary for individuals, private organizations, or other governmental units; and other

trust funds authorized by this Constitution, are not subject to the requirements set forth in paragraph (2) of this subsection.
(4) All cash balances and income of any trust funds abolished under this subsection shall be deposited into the general revenue fund.

(g) Budget Stabilization Fund. Subject to the provisions of this subsection, an amount equal to at least 5% of the last completed fiscal year's net revenue collections for the general revenue fund shall be retained in the budget stabilization fund. The budget stabilization fund's principal balance shall not exceed an amount equal to 10% of the last completed fiscal year's net revenue collections for the general revenue fund. The legislature shall provide criteria for withdrawing funds from the budget stabilization fund in a separate bill for that purpose only and only for the purpose of covering revenue shortfalls of the general revenue fund or for the purpose of providing funding for an emergency, as defined by general law. General law shall provide for the restoration of this fund. The budget stabilization fund shall be comprised of funds not otherwise obligated or committed for any purpose.

(h) Long-Range State Planning Document and Department and Agency Planning Document Processes.
General law shall provide for a long-range state planning document. The governor shall recommend to the legislature biennially any revisions to the long-range state planning document, as defined by law. General law shall require a biennial review and revision of the long-range state planning document and shall require all departments and agencies of state government to develop planning documents that identify statewide strategic goals and objectives, consistent with the long-range state planning document. The long-range state planning document and department and agency planning documents shall remain subject to review and revision by the legislature. The long-range state planning document must include projections of future needs and resources of the state which are consistent with the long-range financial outlook. The department and agency planning documents shall include a

prioritized listing of planned expenditures for review and possible reduction in the event of revenue shortfalls, as defined by general law.

(i) Government Efficiency Task Force. No later than January of 2007, and each fourth year thereafter, the president of the senate, the speaker of the house of representatives, and the governor shall appoint a government efficiency task force, the membership of which shall be established by general law. The task force shall be composed of members of the legislature and representatives from the private and public sectors who shall develop recommendations for improving governmental operations and reducing costs. Staff to assist the task force in performing its duties shall be assigned by general law, and the task force may obtain assistance from the private sector. The task force shall complete its work within one year and shall submit its recommendations to the joint legislative budget commission, the governor, and the chief justice of the supreme court.

(j) Joint Legislative Budget Commission. There is created within the legislature the joint legislative budget commission composed of equal numbers of senate members appointed by the president of the senate and house members appointed by the speaker of the house of representatives. Each member shall serve at the pleasure of the officer who appointed the member. A vacancy on the commission shall be filled in the same manner as the original appointment. From November of each odd-numbered year through October of each even-numbered year, the chairperson of the joint legislative budget commission shall be appointed by the president of the senate and the vice chairperson of the commission shall be appointed by the speaker of the house of representatives. From November of each even-numbered year through October of each odd-numbered year, the chairperson of the joint legislative budget commission shall be appointed by the speaker of the house of representatives and the vice chairperson of the commission shall be appointed by the president of the senate. The joint legislative budget commission shall be governed by the joint rules of the senate and the house of representatives, which shall remain in effect until repealed or amended by concurrent resolution. The commission shall convene at least quarterly and shall convene at the call of the president of the senate and the speaker of the house of representatives. A majority of the commission members of each house plus one additional member from either house constitutes a quorum. Action by the commission requires a majority vote of the commission members present of each house. The commission may conduct its meetings through teleconferences or similar means. In addition to the powers and duties specified in this subsection, the joint legislative budget commission shall exercise all other powers and perform any other duties not in conflict with paragraph (c)(3) and as prescribed by general law or joint rule.

Section 20. Standards for establishing congressional district boundaries In establishing congressional district boundaries:

(a) No apportionment plan or individual district shall be drawn with the intent to favor or disfavor a political party or an incumbent; and districts shall not be drawn with the intent or result of denying or abridging the equal opportunity of racial or language minorities to participate in the political process or to diminish their ability to elect representatives of their choice; and districts shall consist of contiguous territory.
(b) Unless compliance with the standards in this subsection conflicts with the standards in subsection 1(a) or with federal law, districts shall be as nearly equal in population as is practicable; districts shall be compact; and districts shall, where feasible, utilize existing political and geographical boundaries.
(c) The order in which the standards within subsections 1(a) and (b) of this section are set forth shall not be read to establish any priority of one standard over the other within that subsection.
(d) to conform to the format of the State Constitution.

Section 21. Standards for establishing legislative district boundaries In establishing legislative district boundaries:

(a) No apportionment plan or district shall be drawn with the intent to favor or disfavor a political party or an incumbent; and districts shall not be drawn with the intent or result of denying or abridging the equal opportunity of racial or language minorities to participate in the political process or to diminish their ability to elect representatives of their choice; and districts shall consist of contiguous territory.

(b) Unless compliance with the standards in this subsection conflicts with the standards in subsection 1(a) or with federal law, districts shall be as nearly equal in population as is practicable; districts shall be compact; and districts shall, where feasible, utilize existing political and geographical boundaries.

(c) The order in which the standards within subsections 1(a) and (b) of this section are set forth shall not be read to establish any priority of one standard over the other within that subsection.

ARTICLE IV: EXECUTIVE

Section 1. Governor

(a) The supreme executive power shall be vested in a governor, who shall be commander-in-chief of all military forces of the state not in active service of the United States. The governor shall take care that the laws be faithfully executed, commission all officers of the state and counties, and transact all necessary business with the officers of government. The governor may require information in writing from all executive or administrative state, county or municipal officers upon any subject relating to the duties of their respective offices. The governor shall be the chief administrative officer of the state responsible for the planning and budgeting for the state.
(b) The governor may initiate judicial proceedings in the name of the state against any executive or administrative state, county or municipal officer to enforce compliance with any duty or restrain any unauthorized act.
(c) The governor may request in writing the opinion of the justices of the supreme court as to the interpretation of any portion of this constitution upon any question affecting the governor's executive powers and duties. The justices shall, subject to their rules of procedure, permit interested persons to be heard on the questions presented and shall render their written opinion not earlier than ten days from the filing and docketing of the request, unless in their judgment the delay would cause public injury.
(d) The governor shall have power to call out the militia to preserve the public peace, execute the laws of the state, suppress insurrection, or repel invasion.
(e) The governor shall by message at least once in each regular session inform the legislature concerning the condition of the state, propose such reorganization of the executive department as will promote efficiency and economy, and recommend measures in the public interest.

(f) When not otherwise provided for in this constitution, the governor shall fill by appointment any vacancy in state or county office for the remainder of the term of an appointive office, and for the remainder of the term of an elective office if less than twenty-eight months, otherwise until the first Tuesday after the first Monday following the next general election.

Section 2. Lieutenant Governor
There shall be a lieutenant governor, who shall perform such duties pertaining to the office of governor as shall be assigned by the governor, except when otherwise provided by law, and such other duties as may be prescribed by law.

Section 3. Succession to Office of Governor; Acting Governor

(a) Upon vacancy in the office of governor, the lieutenant governor shall become governor. Further succession to the office of governor shall be prescribed by law. A successor shall serve for the remainder of the term.

(b) Upon impeachment of the governor and until completion of trial thereof, or during the governor's physical or mental incapacity, the lieutenant governor shall act as governor. Further succession as acting governor shall be prescribed by law. Incapacity to serve as governor may be determined by the supreme court upon due notice after docketing of a written suggestion thereof by three cabinet members, and in such case restoration of capacity shall be similarly determined after docketing of written suggestion thereof by the governor, the legislature or three cabinet members. Incapacity to serve as governor may also be established by certificate filed with the custodian of state records by the governor declaring incapacity for physical reasons to serve as governor, and in such case restoration of capacity shall be similarly established.

Section 4. Cabinet

(a) There shall be a cabinet composed of an attorney general, a chief financial officer, and a commissioner of agriculture. In addition to the powers and duties specified herein, they shall exercise such powers and perform such duties as may be prescribed by law. In the event of a tie vote of the governor and cabinet, the side on which the governor voted shall be deemed to prevail.

(b) The attorney general shall be the chief state legal officer. There is created in the office of the attorney general the position of statewide prosecutor. The statewide prosecutor shall have concurrent jurisdiction with the state attorneys to prosecute violations of criminal laws occurring or having occurred, in two or more judicial circuits as part of a related transaction, or when any such offense is affecting or has affected two or more judicial circuits as provided by general law. The statewide prosecutor shall be appointed by the attorney general from not less than three persons nominated by the judicial nominating commission for the supreme court, or as otherwise provided by general law.

(c) The chief financial officer shall serve as the chief fiscal officer of the state, and shall settle and approve accounts against the state, and shall keep all state funds and securities.

(d) The commissioner of agriculture shall have supervision of matters pertaining to agriculture except as otherwise provided by law.

(e) The governor as chair, the chief financial officer, and the attorney general shall constitute the state board of administration, which shall succeed to all the power, control, and authority of the state board of administration established pursuant to Article IX, Section 16 of the Constitution of 1885, and which shall continue as a body at least for the life of Article XII, Section 9(c).

(f) The governor as chair, the chief financial officer, the attorney general, and the commissioner of agriculture shall constitute the trustees of the internal improvement trust fund and the land acquisition trust fund as provided by law.

(g) The governor as chair, the chief financial officer, the attorney general, and the commissioner of agriculture shall constitute the agency head of the Department of Law Enforcement.

Section 5. Election of Governor, Lieutenant Governor and Cabinet Members; Qualifications; Terms

(a) At a state-wide general election in each calendar year the number of which is even but not a multiple of four, the electors shall choose a governor and a lieutenant governor and members of the cabinet each for a term of four years beginning on the first Tuesday after the first Monday in January of the succeeding year. In primary elections, candidates for the office of governor may choose to run without a lieutenant governor candidate. In the general election, all candidates for the offices of governor and lieutenant governor shall form joint candidacies in a manner prescribed by law so that each voter shall cast a single vote for a candidate for governor and a candidate for lieutenant governor running together.
(b) When elected, the governor, lieutenant governor and each cabinet member must be an elector not less than thirty years of age who has resided in the state for the preceding seven years. The attorney general must have been a member of the bar of Florida for the preceding five years. No person who has, or but for resignation would have, served as governor or acting governor for more than six years in two consecutive terms shall be elected governor for the succeeding term.

Section 6. Executive Departments

All functions of the executive branch of state government shall be allotted among not more than twenty-five departments, exclusive of those specifically provided for or authorized in this constitution. The administration of each department, unless otherwise provided in this constitution, shall be placed by law under the direct supervision of the governor, the lieutenant governor, the governor and cabinet, a cabinet member, or an officer or board appointed by and serving at the pleasure of the governor, except:

(a) When provided by law, confirmation by the senate or the approval of three members of the cabinet shall be required for appointment to or removal from any designated statutory office.
(b) Boards authorized to grant and revoke licenses to engage in regulated occupations shall be assigned to appropriate departments and their members appointed for fixed terms, subject to removal only for cause.

Section 7. Suspensions; Filling Office During Suspensions

(a) By executive order stating the grounds and filed with the custodian of state records, the governor may suspend from office any state officer not subject to impeachment, any officer of the militia not in the active service of the United States, or any county officer, for malfeasance, misfeasance, neglect of duty, drunkenness, incompetence, permanent inability to perform official duties, or commission of a felony, and may fill the office by appointment for the period of suspension. The suspended officer may at any time before removal be reinstated by the governor.
(b) The senate may, in proceedings prescribed by law, remove from office or reinstate the suspended official and for such purpose the senate may be convened in special session by its president or by a majority of its membership.
(c) By order of the governor any elected municipal officer indicted for crime may be suspended from office until acquitted and the office filled by appointment for the period of suspension, not to extend beyond the term, unless these powers are vested elsewhere by law or the municipal charter.

Section 8. Clemency

(a) Except in cases of treason and in cases where impeachment results in conviction, the governor may, by executive order filed with the custodian of state records, suspend collection of fines and forfeitures, grant reprieves not exceeding sixty days and, with the approval of two members of the cabinet, grant full or conditional pardons, restore civil rights, commute punishment, and remit fines and forfeitures for offenses.

(b) In cases of treason the governor may grant reprieves until adjournment of the regular session of the legislature convening next after the conviction, at which session the legislature may grant a pardon or further reprieve; otherwise the sentence shall be executed.

(c) There may be created by law a parole and probation commission with power to supervise persons on probation and to grant paroles or conditional releases to persons under sentences for crime. The qualifications, method of selection and terms, not to exceed six years, of members of the commission shall be prescribed by law.

Section 9. Fish and Wildlife Conservation Commission

There shall be a fish and wildlife conservation commission, composed of seven members appointed by the governor, subject to confirmation by the senate for staggered terms of five years. The commission shall exercise the regulatory and executive powers of the state with respect to wild animal life and fresh water aquatic life, and shall also exercise regulatory and executive powers of the state with respect to marine life, except that all license fees for taking wild animal life, fresh water aquatic life, and marine life and penalties for violating regulations of the commission shall be prescribed by general law. The commission shall establish procedures to ensure adequate due process in the exercise of its regulatory and executive functions. The legislature may enact laws in aid of the commission, not inconsistent with this section, except that there shall be no special law or general law of local application pertaining to hunting or fishing. The commission's exercise of executive powers in the area of planning, budgeting, personnel management, and purchasing shall be as provided by law. Revenue derived from license fees for the taking of wild animal life and fresh water aquatic life shall be appropriated to the commission by the legislature for the purposes of management, protection, and conservation of wild animal life and fresh water aquatic life. Revenue derived from license fees relating to marine life shall be appropriated by the legislature for the purposes of management, protection, and conservation of marine life as provided by law. The commission shall not be a unit of any other state agency and shall have its own staff, which includes management, research, and enforcement. Unless provided by general law, the commission shall have no authority to regulate matters relating to air and water pollution.

Section 10. Attorney General
The attorney general shall, as directed by general law, request the opinion of the justices of the supreme court as to the validity of any initiative petition circulated pursuant to Section 3 of Article XI. The justices shall, subject to their rules of procedure, permit interested persons to be heard on the questions presented and shall render their written opinion no later than April 1 of the year in which the initiative is to be submitted to the voters pursuant to Section 5 of Article XI.

Section 11. Department of Veterans Affairs
The legislature, by general law, may provide for the establishment of the Department of Veterans Affairs.

Section 12. Department of Elderly Affairs
The legislature may create a Department of Elderly Affairs and prescribe its duties. The provisions governing the administration of the department must comply with Section 6 of Article IV of the State Constitution.

Section 13. Revenue Shortfalls
In the event of revenue shortfalls, as defined by general law, the governor and cabinet may establish all necessary reductions in the state budget in order to comply with the provisions of Article VII, Section 1(d). The governor and cabinet shall implement all necessary reductions for the executive budget, the chief justice of the supreme court shall implement all necessary reductions for the judicial budget, and the speaker of the house of representatives and the president of the senate shall implement all necessary reductions for the legislative budget. Budget reductions pursuant to this section shall be consistent with the

provisions of Article III, Section 19(h).

ARTICLE V: JUDICIARY

Section 1. Courts
The judicial power shall be vested in a supreme court, district courts of appeal, circuit courts and county courts. No other courts may be established by the state, any political subdivision or any municipality. The legislature shall, by general law, divide the state into appellate court districts and judicial circuits following county lines. Commissions established by law, or administrative officers or bodies may be granted quasi-judicial power in matters connected with the functions of their offices. The legislature may establish by general law a civil traffic hearing officer system for the purpose of hearing civil traffic infractions. The legislature may, by general law, authorize a military court-martial to be conducted by military judges of the Florida National Guard, with direct appeal of a decision to the District Court of Appeal, First District.

Section 2. Administration; Practice and Procedure

(a) The supreme court shall adopt rules for the practice and procedure in all courts including the time for seeking appellate review, the administrative supervision of all courts, the transfer to the court having jurisdiction of any proceeding when the jurisdiction of another court has been improvidently invoked, and a requirement that no cause shall be dismissed because an improper remedy has been sought. The supreme court shall adopt rules to allow the court and the district courts of appeal to submit questions relating to military law to the federal Court of Appeals for the Armed Forces for an advisory opinion. Rules of court may be repealed by general law enacted by two-thirds vote of the membership of each house of the legislature.
(b) The chief justice of the supreme court shall be chosen by a majority of the members of the court; shall be the chief administrative officer of the judicial system; and shall have the power to assign justices or judges, including consenting retired justices or judges, to temporary duty in any court for which the judge is qualified and to delegate to a chief judge of a judicial

circuit the power to assign judges for duty in that circuit.

(c) A chief judge for each district court of appeal shall be chosen by a majority of the judges thereof or, if there is no majority, by the chief justice. The chief judge shall be responsible for the administrative supervision of the court.

(d) A chief judge in each circuit shall be chosen from among the circuit judges as provided by supreme court rule. The chief judge shall be responsible for the administrative supervision of the circuit courts and county courts in his circuit.

Section 3. Supreme Court

(a) Organization The supreme court shall consist of seven justices. Of the seven justices, each appellate district shall have at least one justice elected or appointed from the district to the supreme court who is a resident of the district at the time of the original appointment or election. Five justices shall constitute a quorum. The concurrence of four justices shall be necessary to a decision. When recusals for cause would prohibit the court from convening because of the requirements of this section, judges assigned to temporary duty may be substituted for justices.

(b) Jurisdiction

The Supreme Court:

(1) Shall hear appeals from final judgments of trial courts imposing the death penalty and from decisions of district courts of appeal declaring invalid a state statute or a provision of the state constitution.

(2) When provided by general law, shall hear appeals from final judgments entered in proceedings for the validation of bonds or certificates of indebtedness and shall review action of statewide agencies relating to rates or service of utilities providing electric, gas, or telephone service.

(3) May review any decision of a district court of appeal that expressly declares valid a state statute, or that expressly construes a provision of the state or federal constitution, or that expressly affects a class of constitutional or state officers, or that expressly and directly conflicts with a decision of another district court of appeal or of the supreme court on the same question of law.
(4) May review any decision of a district court of appeal that passes upon a question certified by it to be of great public importance, or that is certified by it to be in direct conflict with a decision of another district court of appeal.
(5) May review any order or judgment of a trial court certified by the district court of appeal in which an appeal is pending to be of great public importance, or to have a great effect on the proper administration of justice throughout the state, and certified to require immediate resolution by the supreme court.
(6) May review a question of law certified by the Supreme Court of the United States or a United States Court of Appeals which is determinative of the cause and for which there is no controlling precedent of the supreme court of Florida.
(7) May issue writs of prohibition to courts and all writs necessary to the complete exercise of its jurisdiction.
(8) May issue writs of mandamus and quo warranto to state officers and state agencies.
(9) May, or any justice may, issue writs of habeas corpus returnable before the supreme court or any justice, a district court of appeal or any judge thereof, or any circuit judge.
(10) Shall, when requested by the attorney general pursuant to the provisions of Section 10 of Article IV, render an advisory opinion of the justices, addressing issues as provided by general law.

(c) Clerk And Marshal

The supreme court shall appoint a clerk and a marshal who shall hold office during the pleasure of the court and perform such duties as the court directs. Their compensation shall be fixed by general law. The marshal shall have the power to execute the process of the court throughout the state, and in any county may deputize the sheriff or a deputy sheriff for such purpose.

Section 4. District Courts of Appeal

(a) Organization

There shall be a district court of appeal serving each appellate district. Each district court of appeal shall consist of at least three judges. Three judges shall consider each case and the concurrence of two shall be necessary to a decision.

(b) Jurisdiction

(1) District courts of appeal shall have jurisdiction to hear appeals, that may be taken as a matter of right, from final judgments or orders of trial courts, including those entered on review of administrative action, not directly appealable to the supreme court or a circuit court. They may review interlocutory orders in such cases to the extent provided by rules adopted by the supreme court.
(2) District courts of appeal shall have the power of direct review of administrative action, as prescribed by general law.
(3) A district court of appeal or any judge thereof may issue writs of habeas corpus returnable before the court or any judge thereof or before any circuit judge within the territorial jurisdiction of the court. A district court of appeal may issue writs of mandamus, certiorari, prohibition, quo warranto, and other writs necessary to the complete exercise of its jurisdiction. To the extent necessary to dispose of all issues in a cause properly before it, a district court of appeal may exercise any of the appellate jurisdiction of the circuit courts.

(c) Clerks And Marshals

Each district court of appeal shall appoint a clerk and a marshal who shall hold office during the pleasure of the court and perform such duties as the court directs. Their compensation shall be fixed by general law. The marshal shall have the power to execute the process of the court throughout the territorial jurisdiction of the court, and in any county may deputize the sheriff or a deputy sheriff for such purpose.

Section 5. Circuit Courts

(a) Organization

There shall be a circuit court serving each judicial circuit.

(b) Jurisdiction

The circuit courts shall have original jurisdiction not vested in the county courts, and jurisdiction of appeals when provided by general law. They shall have the power to issue writs of mandamus, quo warranto, certiorari, prohibition and habeas corpus, and all writs necessary or proper to the complete exercise of their jurisdiction. Jurisdiction of the circuit court shall be uniform throughout the state. They shall have the power of direct review of administrative action prescribed by general law.

Section 6. County Courts

(a) Organization

There shall be a county court in each county. There shall be one or more judges for each county court as prescribed by general law.

(b) Jurisdiction

The county courts shall exercise the jurisdiction prescribed by general law. Such jurisdiction shall be uniform throughout the state.

Section 7. Specialized Divisions
All courts except the supreme court may sit in divisions as may be established by general law. A circuit or county court may hold civil and criminal trials and hearings in any place within the territorial jurisdiction of the court as designated by the chief judge of the circuit.

Section 8. Eligibility
No person shall be eligible for office of justice or judge of any court unless the person is an elector of the state and resides in the territorial jurisdiction of the court. No justice or judge shall serve after attaining the age of seventy years except upon temporary assignment or to complete a term, one-half of which has been served. No person is eligible for the office of justice of the supreme court or judge of a district court of appeal unless the person is, and has been for the preceding ten years, a member of the bar of Florida. No person is eligible for the office of circuit judge unless the person is, and has been for the preceding five years, a member of the bar of Florida. Unless otherwise provided by general law, no person is eligible for the office of county court judge unless the person is, and has been for the preceding five years, a member of the bar of Florida. Unless otherwise provided by general law, a person shall be eligible for election or appointment to the office of county court judge in a county having a population of 40,000 or less if the person is a member in good standing of the bar of Florida.

Section 9. Determination of Number of Judges
The supreme court shall establish by rule uniform criteria for the determination of the need for additional judges except supreme court justices, the necessity for decreasing the number of judges and for increasing, decreasing or redefining appellate districts and judicial circuits. If the supreme court finds that a need exists for increasing or decreasing the number of judges or increasing, decreasing or redefining appellate districts and judicial circuits, it shall, prior to the next regular session of the legislature, certify to the legislature its findings and recommendations concerning such need. Upon receipt of such certificate, the legislature, at the

next regular session, shall consider the findings and recommendations and may reject the recommendations or by law implement the recommendations in whole or in part; provided the legislature may create more judicial offices than are recommended by the supreme court or may decrease the number of judicial offices by a greater number than recommended by the court only upon a finding of two-thirds of the membership of both houses of the legislature, that such a need exists. A decrease in the number of judges shall be effective only after the expiration of a term. If the supreme court fails to make findings as provided above when need exists, the legislature may by concurrent resolution request the court to certify its findings and recommendations and upon the failure of the court to certify its findings for nine consecutive months, the legislature may, upon a finding of two-thirds of the membership of both houses of the legislature that a need exists, increase or decrease the number of judges or increase, decrease or redefine appellate districts and judicial circuits.

Section 10. Retention; Election and Terms

(a) Any justice or judge may qualify for retention by a vote of the electors in the general election next preceding the expiration of the justice's or judge's term in the manner prescribed by law. If a justice or judge is ineligible or fails to qualify for retention, a vacancy shall exist in that office upon the expiration of the term being served by the justice or judge. When a justice or judge so qualifies, the ballot shall read substantially as follows: "Shall Justice (or Judge) (name of justice or judge) of the (name of the court) be retained in office?" If a majority of the qualified electors voting within the territorial jurisdiction of the court vote to retain, the justice or judge shall be retained for a term of six years. The term of the justice or judge retained shall commence on the first Tuesday after the first Monday in January following the general election. If a majority of the qualified electors voting within the territorial jurisdiction of the court vote to not retain, a vacancy shall exist in that office upon the expiration of the term being served by the justice or judge.

(b)(1) The election of circuit judges shall be preserved notwithstanding the provisions of subsection (a) unless a majority of those voting in the jurisdiction of that circuit approves a local option to select circuit judges by merit selection and retention rather than by election. The election of circuit judges shall be by a vote of the qualified electors within the territorial jurisdiction of the court.

(2) The election of county court judges shall be preserved notwithstanding the provisions of subsection (a) unless a majority of those voting in the jurisdiction of that county approves a local option to select county judges by merit selection and retention rather than by election. The election of county court judges shall be by a vote of the qualified electors within the territorial jurisdiction of the court.

(3)a. A vote to exercise a local option to select circuit court judges and county court judges by merit selection and retention rather than by election shall be held in each circuit and county at the general election in the year 2000. If a vote to exercise this local option fails in a vote of the electors, such option shall not again be put to a vote of the electors of that jurisdiction until the expiration of at least two years.
b. After the year 2000, a circuit may initiate the local option for merit selection and retention or the election of circuit judges, whichever is applicable, by filing with the custodian of state records a petition signed by the number of electors equal to at least ten percent of the votes cast in the circuit in the last preceding election in which presidential electors were chosen.
c. After the year 2000, a county may initiate the local option for merit selection and retention or the election of county court judges, whichever is applicable, by filing with the supervisor of elections a petition signed by the number of electors equal to at least ten percent of the votes cast in the county in the last preceding election in which presidential electors were chosen.

The terms of circuit judges and judges of county courts shall be for six years.

Section 11. Vacancies

(a) Whenever a vacancy occurs in a judicial office to which election for retention applies, the governor shall fill the vacancy by appointing for a term ending on the first Tuesday after the first Monday in January of the year following the next general election occurring at least one year after the date of appointment, one of not fewer than three persons nor more than six persons nominated by the appropriate judicial nominating commission.
(b) The governor shall fill each vacancy on a circuit court or on a county court, wherein the judges are elected by a majority vote of the electors, by appointing for a term ending on the first Tuesday after the first Monday in January of the year following the next primary and general election occurring at least one year after the date of appointment, one of not fewer than three persons nor more than six persons nominated by the appropriate judicial nominating commission. An election shall be held to fill that judicial office for the term of the office beginning at the end of the appointed term.
(c) The nominations shall be made within thirty days from the occurrence of a vacancy unless the period is extended by the governor for a time not to exceed thirty days. The governor shall make the appointment within sixty days after the nominations have been certified to the governor.
(d) There shall be a separate judicial nominating commission as provided by general law for the supreme court, each district court of appeal, and each judicial circuit for all trial courts within the circuit. Uniform rules of procedure shall be established by the judicial nominating commissions at each level of the court system. Such rules, or any part thereof, may be repealed by general law enacted by a majority vote of the membership of each house of the legislature, or by the supreme court, five justices concurring. Except for deliberations of the judicial nominating commissions, the proceedings of the commissions and their records shall be open to the public.

Section 12. Discipline; Removal and Retirement

(a) Judicial Qualifications Commission
A judicial qualifications commission is created.

(1) There shall be a judicial qualifications commission vested with jurisdiction to investigate and recommend to the Supreme Court of Florida the removal from office of any justice or judge whose conduct, during term of office or otherwise occurring on or after November 1, 1966, (without regard to the effective date of this section) demonstrates a present unfitness to hold office, and to investigate and recommend the discipline of a justice or judge whose conduct, during term of office or otherwise occurring on or after November 1, 1966 (without regard to the effective date of this section), warrants such discipline. For purposes of this section, discipline is defined as any or all of the following: reprimand, fine, suspension with or without pay, or lawyer discipline. The commission shall have jurisdiction over justices and judges regarding allegations that misconduct occurred before or during service as a justice or judge if a complaint is made no later than one year following service as a justice or judge. The commission shall have jurisdiction regarding allegations of incapacity during service as a justice or judge. The commission shall be composed of:

a. Two judges of district courts of appeal selected by the judges of those courts, two circuit judges selected by the judges of the circuit courts and two judges of county courts selected by the judges of those courts;
b. Four electors who reside in the state, who are members of the bar of Florida, and who shall be chosen by the governing body of the bar of Florida; and
c. Five electors who reside in the state, who have never held judicial office or been members of the bar of Florida, and who shall be appointed by the governor.

(2) The members of the judicial qualifications commission shall serve staggered terms, not to exceed six years, as prescribed by general law. No member of the commission except a judge shall be eligible for state judicial office while acting as a member of the commission and for a period of two years thereafter. No member of the commission shall hold office in a political party or participate in any campaign for judicial office or hold public office; provided that a judge may campaign for judicial office and hold that office. The commission shall elect one of its members as its chairperson.

(3) Members of the judicial qualifications commission not subject to impeachment shall be subject to removal from the commission pursuant to the provisions of Article IV, Section 7, Florida Constitution.

(4) The commission shall adopt rules regulating its proceedings, the filling of vacancies by the appointing authorities, the disqualification of members, the rotation of members between the panels, and the temporary replacement of disqualified or incapacitated members. The commission's rules, or any part thereof, may be repealed by general law enacted by a majority vote of the membership of each house of the legislature, or by the supreme court, five justices concurring. The commission shall have power to issue subpoenas. Until formal charges against a justice or judge are filed by the investigative panel with the clerk of the supreme court of Florida all proceedings by or before the commission shall be confidential; provided, however, upon a finding of probable cause and the filing by the investigative panel with said clerk of such formal charges against a justice or judge such charges and all further proceedings before the commission shall be public.

(5) The commission shall have access to all information from all executive, legislative and judicial agencies, including grand juries, subject to the rules of the commission. At any time, on request of the speaker of the house of representatives or the governor, the commission shall make available all information in the possession of the commission for use in consideration of impeachment or suspension, respectively.

(b) Panels

The commission shall be divided into an investigative panel and a hearing panel as established by rule of the commission. The investigative panel is vested with the jurisdiction to receive or initiate complaints, conduct investigations, dismiss complaints, and upon a vote of a simple majority of the panel submit formal charges to the hearing panel. The hearing panel is vested with the authority to receive and hear formal charges from the investigative panel and upon a two-thirds vote of the panel recommend to the supreme court the removal of a justice or judge or the involuntary retirement of a justice or judge for any permanent disability that seriously interferes with the performance of judicial duties. Upon a simple majority vote of the membership of the hearing panel, the panel may recommend to the supreme court that the justice or judge be subject to appropriate discipline.

(c) Supreme Court

The supreme court shall receive recommendations from the judicial qualifications commission's hearing panel.

(1) The supreme court may accept, reject, or modify in whole or in part the findings, conclusions, and recommendations of the commission and it may order that the justice or judge be subjected to appropriate discipline, or be removed from office with termination of compensation for willful or persistent failure to perform judicial duties or for other conduct unbecoming a member of the judiciary demonstrating a present unfitness to hold office, or be involuntarily retired for any permanent disability that seriously interferes with the performance of judicial duties. Malafides, scienter or moral turpitude on the part of a justice or judge shall not be required for removal from office of a justice or judge whose conduct demonstrates a present unfitness to hold office. After the filing of a formal proceeding and upon request of the investigative panel, the supreme court may suspend the justice or judge from office, with or without compensation, pending final determination of the inquiry.

(2) The supreme court may award costs to the prevailing party.

(d) The power of removal conferred by this section shall be both alternative and cumulative to the power of impeachment.
(e) Notwithstanding any of the foregoing provisions of this section, if the person who is the subject of proceedings by the judicial qualifications commission is a justice of the supreme court of Florida all justices of such court automatically shall be disqualified to sit as justices of such court with respect to all proceedings therein concerning such person and the supreme court for such purposes shall be composed of a panel consisting of the seven chief judges of the judicial circuits of the state of Florida most senior in tenure of judicial office as circuit judge. For purposes of determining seniority of such circuit judges in the event there be judges of equal tenure in judicial office as circuit judge the judge or judges from the lower numbered circuit or circuits shall be deemed senior. In the event any such chief circuit judge is under investigation by the judicial qualifications commission or is otherwise disqualified or unable to serve on the panel, the next most senior chief circuit judge or judges shall serve in place of such disqualified or disabled chief circuit judge.

(f) Schedule to Section 12

(1) Except to the extent inconsistent with the provisions of this section, all provisions of law and rules of court in force on the effective date of this article shall continue in effect until superseded in the manner authorized by the constitution.
(2) After this section becomes effective and until adopted by rule of the commission consistent with it:

a. The commission shall be divided, as determined by the chairperson, into one investigative panel and one hearing panel to meet the responsibilities set forth in this section.

b. The investigative panel shall be composed of:

1. Four judges,
2. Two members of the bar of Florida, and
3. Three non-lawyers.

c. The hearing panel shall be composed of:

1. Two judges,
2. Two members of the bar of Florida, and
3. Two non-lawyers.

d. Membership on the panels may rotate in a manner determined by the rules of the commission provided that no member shall vote as a member of the investigative and hearing panel on the same proceeding.

e. The commission shall hire separate staff for each panel.

f. The members of the commission shall serve for staggered terms of six years.

g. The terms of office of the present members of the judicial qualifications commission shall expire upon the effective date of the amendments to this section approved by the legislature during the regular session of the legislature in 1996 and new members shall be appointed to serve the following staggered terms:

1. Group I
The terms of five members, composed of two electors as set forth in s. 12(a)(1)c. of Article V, one member of the bar of Florida as set forth in s. 12(a)(1)b. of Article V, one judge from the district courts of appeal and one circuit judge as set forth in s. 12(a)(1)a. of Article V, shall expire on December 31, 1998.

2. Group II
The terms of five members, composed of one elector as set forth in s. 12(a)(1)c. of Article V, two members of the bar of Florida as set forth in s. 12(a)(1)b. of Article V, one circuit judge and one county judge as set forth in s. 12(a)(1)a. of Article V shall expire

on December 31, 2000.

3. Group III
The terms of five members, composed of two electors as set forth in s. 12(a)(1)c. of Article V, one member of the bar of Florida as set forth in s. 12(a)(1)b., one judge from the district courts of appeal and one county judge as set forth in s. 12(a)(1)a. of Article V, shall expire on December 31, 2002.

h. An appointment to fill a vacancy of the commission shall be for the remainder of the term.
i. Selection of members by district courts of appeal judges, circuit judges, and county court judges, shall be by no less than a majority of the members voting at the respective courts' conferences. Selection of members by the board of governors of the bar of Florida shall be by no less than a majority of the board.
j. The commission shall be entitled to recover the costs of investigation and prosecution, in addition to any penalty levied by the supreme court.
k. The compensation of members and referees shall be the travel expenses or transportation and per diem allowance as provided by general law.

Section 13. Prohibited Activities
All justices and judges shall devote full time to their judicial duties. They shall not engage in the practice of law or hold office in any political party.

Section 14. Funding

(a) All justices and judges shall be compensated only by state salaries fixed by general law. Funding for the state courts system, state attorneys' offices, public defenders' offices, and court-appointed counsel, except as otherwise provided in subsection (c), shall be provided from state revenues appropriated by general law.

(b) All funding for the offices of the clerks of the circuit and county courts performing court-related functions, except as otherwise provided in this subsection and subsection (c), shall be provided by adequate and appropriate filing fees for judicial proceedings and service charges and costs for performing court-related functions as required by general law. Selected salaries, costs, and expenses of the state courts system may be funded from appropriate filing fees for judicial proceedings and service charges and costs for performing court-related functions, as provided by general law. Where the requirements of either the United States Constitution or the Constitution of the State of Florida preclude the imposition of filing fees for judicial proceedings and service charges and costs for performing court-related functions sufficient to fund the court-related functions of the offices of the clerks of the circuit and county courts, the state shall provide, as determined by the legislature, adequate and appropriate supplemental funding from state revenues appropriated by general law.

(c) No county or municipality, except as provided in this subsection, shall be required to provide any funding for the state courts system, state attorneys' offices, public defenders' offices, court-appointed counsel or the offices of the clerks of the circuit and county courts performing court-related functions. Counties shall be required to fund the cost of communications services, existing radio systems, existing multi-agency criminal justice information systems, and the cost of construction or lease, maintenance, utilities, and security of facilities for the trial courts, public defenders' offices, state attorneys' offices, and the offices of the clerks of the circuit and county courts performing court-related functions. Counties shall also pay reasonable and necessary salaries, costs, and expenses of the state courts system to meet local requirements as determined by general law.

(d) The judiciary shall have no power to fix appropriations.

Section 15. Attorneys; Admission and Discipline
The supreme court shall have exclusive jurisdiction to regulate the admission of persons to the practice of law and the discipline of persons admitted.

Section 16. Clerks of the Circuit Courts
There shall be in each county a clerk of the circuit court who shall be selected pursuant to the provisions of Article VIII section 1. Notwithstanding any other provision of the constitution, the duties of the clerk of the circuit court may be divided by special or general law between two officers, one serving as clerk of court and one serving as ex officio clerk of the board of county commissioners, auditor, recorder, and custodian of all county funds. There may be a clerk of the county court if authorized by general or special law.

Section 17. State Attorneys
In each judicial circuit a state attorney shall be elected for a term of four years. Except as otherwise provided in this constitution, the state attorney shall be the prosecuting officer of all trial courts in that circuit and shall perform other duties prescribed by general law; provided, however, when authorized by general law, the violations of all municipal ordinances may be prosecuted by municipal prosecutors. A state attorney shall be an elector of the state and reside in the territorial jurisdiction of the circuit; shall be and have been a member of the bar of Florida for the preceding five years; shall devote full time to the duties of the office; and shall not engage in the private practice of law. State attorneys shall appoint such assistant state attorneys as may be authorized by law.

Section 18. Public Defenders
In each judicial circuit a public defender shall be elected for a term of four years, who shall perform duties prescribed by general law. A public defender shall be an elector of the state and reside in the territorial jurisdiction of the circuit and shall be and have been a member of the Bar of Florida for the preceding five years. Public defenders shall appoint such assistant public

defenders as may be authorized by law.

Section 19. Judicial Officers as Conservators of the Peace

All judicial officers in this state shall be conservators of the peace.

Section 20. Schedule to Article V

(a) This article shall replace all of Article V of the Constitution of 1885, as amended, which shall then stand repealed.
(b) Except to the extent inconsistent with the provisions of this article, all provisions of law and rules of court in force on the effective date of this article shall continue in effect until superseded in the manner authorized by the constitution.
(c) After this article becomes effective, and until changed by general law consistent with sections 1 through 19 of this article:

(1) The supreme court shall have the jurisdiction immediately theretofore exercised by it, and it shall determine all proceedings pending before it on the effective date of this article.
(2) The appellate districts shall be those in existence on the date of adoption of this article. There shall be a district court of appeal in each district. The district courts of appeal shall have the jurisdiction immediately theretofore exercised by the district courts of appeal and shall determine all proceedings pending before them on the effective date of this article.
(3) Circuit courts shall have jurisdiction of appeals from county courts and municipal courts, except those appeals which may be taken directly to the supreme court; and they shall have exclusive original jurisdiction in all actions at law not cognizable by the county courts; of proceedings relating to the settlement of the estate of decedents and minors, the granting of letters testamentary, guardianship, involuntary hospitalization, the determination of incompetency, and other jurisdiction usually pertaining to courts of probate; in all cases in equity including all cases relating to juveniles; of all felonies and of all misdemeanors arising out of the same circumstances as a felony which is also charged; in all cases involving legality of any tax

assessment or toll; in the action of ejectment; and in all actions involving the titles or boundaries or right of possession of real property. The circuit court may issue injunctions. There shall be judicial circuits which shall be the judicial circuits in existence on the date of adoption of this article. The chief judge of a circuit may authorize a county court judge to order emergency hospitalizations pursuant to Chapter 71-131, Laws of Florida, in the absence from the county of the circuit judge and the county court judge shall have the power to issue all temporary orders and temporary injunctions necessary or proper to the complete exercise of such jurisdiction.

(4) County courts shall have original jurisdiction in all criminal misdemeanor cases not cognizable by the circuit courts, of all violations of municipal and county ordinances, and of all actions at law in which the matter in controversy does not exceed the sum of two thousand five hundred dollars ($2,500.00) exclusive of interest and costs, except those within the exclusive jurisdiction of the circuit courts. Judges of county courts shall be committing magistrates. The county courts shall have jurisdiction now exercised by the county judge's courts other than that vested in the circuit court by subsection (c)(3) hereof, the jurisdiction now exercised by the county courts, the claims court, the small claims courts, the small claims magistrates courts, magistrates courts, justice of the peace courts, municipal courts and courts of chartered counties, including but not limited to the counties referred to in Article VIII, sections 9, 10, 11 and 24 of the Constitution of 1885.

(5) Each judicial nominating commission shall be composed of the following:

a. Three members appointed by the Board of Governors of The Florida Bar from among The Florida Bar members who are actively engaged in the practice of law with offices within the territorial jurisdiction of the affected court, district or circuit;
b. Three electors who reside in the territorial jurisdiction of the court or circuit appointed by the governor; and

c. Three electors who reside in the territorial jurisdiction of the court or circuit and who are not members of the bar of Florida, selected and appointed by a majority vote of the other six members of the commission.

(6) No justice or judge shall be a member of a judicial nominating commission. A member of a judicial nominating commission may hold public office other than judicial office. No member shall be eligible for appointment to state judicial office so long as that person is a member of a judicial nominating commission and for a period of two years thereafter. All acts of a judicial nominating commission shall be made with a concurrence of a majority of its members.

(7) The members of a judicial nominating commission shall serve for a term of four years except the terms of the initial members of the judicial nominating commissions shall expire as follows:

a. The terms of one member of category a. b. and c. in subsection (c)(5) hereof shall expire on July 1, 1974;
b. The terms of one member of category a. b. and c. in subsection (c)(5) hereof shall expire on July 1, 1975;
c. The terms of one member of category a. b. and c. in subsection (c)(5) hereof shall expire on July 1, 1976;

(8) All fines and forfeitures arising from offenses tried in the county court shall be collected, and accounted for by clerk of the court, and deposited in a special trust account. All fines and forfeitures received from violations of ordinances or misdemeanors committed within a county or municipal ordinances committed within a municipality within the territorial jurisdiction of the county court shall be paid monthly to the county or municipality respectively. If any costs are assessed and collected in connection with offenses tried in county court, all court costs shall be paid into the general revenue fund of the state of Florida and such other funds as prescribed by general law.

(9) Any municipality or county may apply to the chief judge of the circuit in which that municipality or county is situated for the county court to sit in a location suitable to the municipality or county and convenient in time and place to its citizens and police officers and upon such application said chief judge shall direct the court to sit in the location unless the chief judge shall determine the request is not justified. If the chief judge does not authorize the county court to sit in the location requested, the county or municipality may apply to the supreme court for an order directing the county court to sit in the location. Any municipality or county which so applies shall be required to provide the appropriate physical facilities in which the county court may hold court.

(10) All courts except the supreme court may sit in divisions as may be established by local rule approved by the supreme court.

(11) A county court judge in any county having a population of 40,000 or less according to the last decennial census, shall not be required to be a member of the bar of Florida.

(12) Municipal prosecutors may prosecute violations of municipal ordinances.

(13) Justice shall mean a justice elected or appointed to the supreme court and shall not include any judge assigned from any court.

(d) When this article becomes effective:

(1) All courts not herein authorized, except as provided by subsection (d)(4) of this section shall cease to exist and jurisdiction to conclude all pending cases and enforce all prior orders and judgments shall vest in the court that would have jurisdiction of the cause if thereafter instituted. All records of and property held by courts abolished hereby shall be transferred to the proper office of the appropriate court under this article.

(2) Judges of the following courts, if their terms do not expire in 1973 and if they are eligible under subsection (d)(8) hereof, shall become additional judges of the circuit court for each of the counties of their respective circuits, and shall serve as such circuit judges for the remainder of the terms to which they were elected and shall be eligible for election as circuit judges thereafter. These courts are: civil court of record of Dade county, all criminal courts of record, the felony courts of record of Alachua, Leon and Volusia Counties, the courts of record of Broward, Brevard, Escambia, Hillsborough, Lee, Manatee and Sarasota Counties, the civil and criminal court of record of Pinellas County, and county judge's courts and separate juvenile courts in counties having a population in excess of 100,000 according to the 1970 federal census. On the effective date of this article, there shall be an additional number of positions of circuit judges equal to the number of existing circuit judges and the number of judges of the above named courts whose term expires in 1973. Elections to such offices shall take place at the same time and manner as elections to other state judicial offices in 1972 and the terms of such offices shall be for a term of six years. Unless changed pursuant to section nine of this article, the number of circuit judges presently existing and created by this subsection shall not be changed.

(3) In all counties having a population of less than 100,000 according to the 1970 federal census and having more than one county judge on the date of the adoption of this article, there shall be the same number of judges of the county court as there are county judges existing on that date unless changed pursuant to section 9 of this article.

(4) Municipal courts shall continue with their same jurisdiction until amended or terminated in a manner prescribed by special or general law or ordinances, or until January 3, 1977, whichever occurs first. On that date all municipal courts not previously abolished shall cease to exist. Judges of municipal courts shall remain in office and be subject to reappointment or reelection in the manner prescribed by law until said courts are terminated pursuant to the provisions of this subsection. Upon municipal courts being terminated or abolished in accordance with the provisions of this subsection, the judges thereof who are not members of the bar of Florida, shall be eligible to seek election as judges of county courts of their respective counties.

(5) Judges, holding elective office in all other courts abolished by this article, whose terms do not expire in 1973 including judges established pursuant to Article VIII, sections 9 and 11 of the Constitution of 1885 shall serve as judges of the county court for the remainder of the term to which they were elected. Unless created pursuant to section 9, of this Article V such judicial office shall not continue to exist thereafter.

(6) By March 21, 1972, the supreme court shall certify the need for additional circuit and county judges. The legislature in the 1972 regular session may by general law create additional offices of judge, the terms of which shall begin on the effective date of this article. Elections to such offices shall take place at the same time and manner as election to other state judicial offices in 1972.

(7) County judges of existing county judge's courts and justices of the peace and magistrates' court who are not members of bar of Florida shall be eligible to seek election as county court judges of their respective counties.

(8) No judge of a court abolished by this article shall become or be eligible to become a judge of the circuit court unless the judge has been a member of bar of Florida for the preceding five years.

(9) The office of judges of all other courts abolished by this article shall be abolished as of the effective date of this article.

(10) The offices of county solicitor and prosecuting attorney shall stand abolished, and all county solicitors and prosecuting attorneys holding such offices upon the effective date of this article shall become and serve as assistant state attorneys for the circuits in which their counties are situate for the remainder of their terms, with compensation not less than that received immediately before the effective date of this article.

(e) **Limited Operation of Some Provisions**

(1) All justices of the supreme court, judges of the district courts of appeal and circuit judges in office upon the effective date of this article shall retain their offices for the remainder of their respective terms. All members of the judicial qualifications commission in office upon the effective date of this article shall retain their offices for the remainder of their respective terms. Each state attorney in office on the effective date of this article shall retain the office for the remainder of the term.

(2) No justice or judge holding office immediately after this article becomes effective who held judicial office on July 1, 1957, shall be subject to retirement from judicial office because of age pursuant to section 8 of this article.

(f) Until otherwise provided by law, the nonjudicial duties required of county judges shall be performed by the judges of the county court.

(g) All provisions of Article V of the Constitution of 1885, as amended, not embraced herein which are not inconsistent with this revision shall become statutes subject to modification or repeal as are other statutes.

(h) The requirements of section 14 relative to all county court judges or any judge of a municipal court who continues to hold office pursuant to subsection (d)(4) hereof being compensated by state salaries shall not apply prior to January 3, 1977, unless otherwise provided by general law.

(i) Deletion of Obsolete Schedule Items
The legislature shall have power, by concurrent resolution, to delete from this article any subsection of this section 20 including this subsection, when all events to which the subsection to be deleted is or could become applicable have occurred. A legislative determination of fact made as a basis for application of this subsection shall be subject to judicial review.

(j) Effective Date
Unless otherwise provided herein, this article shall become effective at 11:59 o'clock P.M., Eastern Standard Time, January 1, 1973.

ARTICLE VI: SUFFRAGE AND ELECTIONS

Section 1. Regulation of Elections
All elections by the people shall be by direct and secret vote. General elections shall be determined by a plurality of votes cast. Registration and elections shall, and political party functions may, be regulated by law; however, the requirements for a candidate with no party affiliation or for a candidate of a minor party for placement of the candidate's name on the ballot shall be no greater than the requirements for a candidate of the party having the largest number of registered voters.

Section 2. Electors
Every citizen of the United States who is at least eighteen years of age and who is a permanent resident of the state, if registered as provided by law, shall be an elector of the county where registered.

Section 3. Oath
Each eligible citizen upon registering shall subscribe the following: "I do solemnly swear (or affirm) that I will protect and defend the Constitution of the United States and the Constitution of the State of Florida, and that I am qualified to register as an elector under the Constitution and laws of the State of Florida."

Section 4. Disqualifications

(a) No person convicted of a felony, or adjudicated in this or any other state to be mentally incompetent, shall be qualified to vote or hold office until restoration of civil rights or removal of disability.
(b) No person may appear on the ballot for re-election to any of the following offices:

(1) Florida representative,
(2) Florida senator,
(3) Florida Lieutenant governor,
(4) any office of the Florida cabinet,

(5) U.S. Representative from Florida, or
(6) U.S. Senator from Florida

if, by the end of the current term of office, the person will have served (or, but for resignation, would have served) in that office for eight consecutive years.

Section 5. Primary, General, and Special Elections

(a) A general election shall be held in each county on the first Tuesday after the first Monday in November of each even-numbered year to choose a successor to each elective state and county officer whose term will expire before the next general election and, except as provided herein, to fill each vacancy in elective office for the unexpired portion of the term. A general election may be suspended or delayed due to a state of emergency or impending emergency pursuant to general law. Special elections and referenda shall be held as provided by law.
(b) If all candidates for an office have the same party affiliation and the winner will have no opposition in the general election, all qualified electors, regardless of party affiliation, may vote in the primary elections for that office.

Section 6. Municipal and District Elections
Registration and elections in municipalities shall, and in other governmental entities created by statute may, be provided by law.

Section 7. Campaign Spending Limits and Funding of Campaigns for Elective State-Wide Office
It is the policy of this state to provide for state-wide elections in which all qualified candidates may compete effectively. A method of public financing for campaigns for state-wide office shall be established by law. Spending limits shall be established for such campaigns for candidates who use public funds in their campaigns. The legislature shall provide funding for this provision. General law implementing this paragraph shall be at least as protective of effective competition by a candidate who

uses public funds as the general law in effect on January 1, 1998.

ARTICLE VII: FINANCE AND TAXATION

Section 1. Taxation; Appropriations; State Expenses; State Revenue Limitation

(a) No tax shall be levied except in pursuance of law. No state ad valorem taxes shall be levied upon real estate or tangible personal property. All other forms of taxation shall be preempted to the state except as provided by general law.
(b) Motor vehicles, boats, airplanes, trailers, trailer coaches and mobile homes, as defined by law, shall be subject to a license tax for their operation in the amounts and for the purposes prescribed by law, but shall not be subject to ad valorem taxes.
(c) No money shall be drawn from the treasury except in pursuance of appropriation made by law.
(d) Provision shall be made by law for raising sufficient revenue to defray the expenses of the state for each fiscal period.
(e) Except as provided herein, state revenues collected for any fiscal year shall be limited to state revenues allowed under this subsection for the prior fiscal year plus an adjustment for growth. As used in this subsection, "growth" means an amount equal to the average annual rate of growth in Florida personal income over the most recent twenty quarters times the state revenues allowed under this subsection for the prior fiscal year. For the 1995-1996 fiscal year, the state revenues allowed under this subsection for the prior fiscal year shall equal the state revenues collected for the 1994-1995 fiscal year. Florida personal income shall be determined by the legislature, from information available from the United States Department of Commerce or its successor on the first day of February prior to the beginning of the fiscal year. State revenues collected for any fiscal year in excess of this limitation shall be transferred to the budget stabilization fund until the fund reaches the maximum balance specified in Section 19(g) of Article III, and thereafter shall be refunded to taxpayers as provided by general law. State revenues allowed under this subsection for any fiscal year may be increased by a two-thirds vote of the membership of each house of the legislature in a separate bill that contains no other

subject and that sets forth the dollar amount by which the state revenues allowed will be increased. The vote may not be taken less than seventy-two hours after the third reading of the bill. For purposes of this subsection, "state revenues" means taxes, fees, licenses, and charges for services imposed by the legislature on individuals, businesses, or agencies outside state government. However, "state revenues" does not include: revenues that are necessary to meet the requirements set forth in documents authorizing the issuance of bonds by the state; revenues that are used to provide matching funds for the federal Medicaid program with the exception of the revenues used to support the Public Medical Assistance Trust Fund or its successor program and with the exception of state matching funds used to fund elective expansions made after July 1, 1994; proceeds from the state lottery returned as prizes; receipts of the Florida Hurricane Catastrophe Fund; balances carried forward from prior fiscal years; taxes, licenses, fees, and charges for services imposed by local, regional, or school district governing bodies; or revenue from taxes, licenses, fees, and charges for services required to be imposed by any amendment or revision to this constitution after July 1, 1994. An adjustment to the revenue limitation shall be made by general law to reflect the fiscal impact of transfers of responsibility for the funding of governmental functions between the state and other levels of government. The legislature shall, by general law, prescribe procedures necessary to administer this subsection.

Section 2. Taxes; Rate
All ad valorem taxation shall be at a uniform rate within each taxing unit, except the taxes on intangible personal property may be at different rates but shall never exceed two mills on the dollar of assessed value; provided, as to any obligations secured by mortgage, deed of trust, or other lien on real estate wherever located, an intangible tax of not more than two mills on the dollar may be levied by law to be in lieu of all other intangible assessments on such obligations.

Section 3. Taxes; Exemptions

(a) All property owned by a municipality and used exclusively by it for municipal or public purposes shall be exempt from taxation. A municipality, owning property outside the municipality, may be required by general law to make payment to the taxing unit in which the property is located. Such portions of property as are used predominantly for educational, literary, scientific, religious or charitable purposes may be exempted by general law from taxation.

(b) There shall be exempt from taxation, cumulatively, to every head of a family residing in this state, household goods and personal effects to the value fixed by general law, not less than one thousand dollars, and to every widow or widower or person who is blind or totally and permanently disabled, property to the value fixed by general law not less than five hundred dollars.

(c) Any county or municipality may, for the purpose of its respective tax levy and subject to the provisions of this subsection and general law, grant community and economic development ad valorem tax exemptions to new businesses and expansions of existing businesses, as defined by general law. Such an exemption may be granted only by ordinance of the county or municipality, and only after the electors of the county or municipality voting on such question in a referendum authorize the county or municipality to adopt such ordinances. An exemption so granted shall apply to improvements to real property made by or for the use of a new business and improvements to real property related to the expansion of an existing business and shall also apply to tangible personal property of such new business and tangible personal property related to the expansion of an existing business. The amount or limits of the amount of such exemption shall be specified by general law. The period of time for which such exemption may be granted to a new business or expansion of an existing business shall be determined by general law. The authority to grant such exemption shall expire ten years from the date of approval by the electors of the county or municipality, and may be renewable by referendum as provided by general law.

(d) Any county or municipality may, for the purpose of its respective tax levy and subject to the provisions of this subsection and general law, grant historic preservation ad valorem tax exemptions to owners of historic properties. This exemption may be granted only by ordinance of the county or municipality. The amount or limits of the amount of this exemption and the requirements for eligible properties must be specified by general law. The period of time for which this exemption may be granted to a property owner shall be determined by general law.

(e) By general law and subject to conditions specified therein:
(1) Twenty-five thousand dollars of the assessed value of property subject to tangible personal property tax shall be exempt from ad valorem taxation.
(2) The assessed value of solar devices or renewable energy source devices subject to tangible personal property tax may be exempt from ad valorem taxation, subject to limitations provided by general law.

(f) There shall be granted an ad valorem tax exemption for real property dedicated in perpetuity for conservation purposes, including real property encumbered by perpetual conservation easements or by other perpetual conservation protections, as defined by general law.

(g) By general law and subject to the conditions specified therein, each person who receives a homestead exemption as provided in section 6 of this article; who was a member of the United States military or military reserves, the United States Coast Guard or its reserves, or the Florida National Guard; and who was deployed during the preceding calendar year on active duty outside the continental United States, Alaska, or Hawaii in support of military operations designated by the legislature shall receive an additional exemption equal to a percentage of the taxable value of his or her homestead property. The applicable percentage shall be calculated as the number of days during the preceding calendar year the person was deployed on active duty outside the continental United States, Alaska, or Hawaii in support of military operations designated by the legislature divided by the number of days in that year.

Section 4. Taxation; Assessments
By general law regulations shall be prescribed which shall secure a just valuation of all property for ad valorem taxation, provided:

(a) Agricultural land, land producing high water recharge to Florida's aquifers, or land used exclusively for noncommercial recreational purposes may be classified by general law and assessed solely on the basis of character or use.
(b) As provided by general law and subject to conditions, limitations, and reasonable definitions specified therein, land used for conservation purposes shall be classified by general law and assessed solely on the basis of character or use.
(c) Pursuant to general law tangible personal property held for sale as stock in trade and livestock may be valued for taxation at a specified percentage of its value, may be classified for tax purposes, or may be exempted from taxation.
(d) All persons entitled to a homestead exemption under Section 6 of this Article shall have their homestead assessed at just value as of January 1 of the year following the effective date of this amendment. This assessment shall change only as provided in this subsection.

(1) Assessments subject to this subsection shall be changed annually on January 1st of each year; but those changes in assessments shall not exceed the lower of the following:
a. Three percent (3%) of the assessment for the prior year.
b. The percent change in the Consumer Price Index for all urban consumers, U.S. City Average, all items 1967=100, or successor reports for the preceding calendar year as initially reported by the United States Department of Labor, Bureau of Labor Statistics.
(2) No assessment shall exceed just value.

(3) After any change of ownership, as provided by general law, homestead property shall be assessed at just value as of January 1 of the following year, unless the provisions of paragraph (8) apply. Thereafter, the homestead shall be assessed as provided in this subsection.

(4) New homestead property shall be assessed at just value as of January 1st of the year following the establishment of the homestead, unless the provisions of paragraph (8) apply. That assessment shall only change as provided in this subsection.

(5) Changes, additions, reductions, or improvements to homestead property shall be assessed as provided for by general law; provided, however, after the adjustment for any change, addition, reduction, or improvement, the property shall be assessed as provided in this subsection.

(6) In the event of a termination of homestead status, the property shall be assessed as provided by general law.

(7) The provisions of this amendment are severable. If any of the provisions of this amendment shall be held unconstitutional by any court of competent jurisdiction, the decision of such court shall not affect or impair any remaining provisions of this amendment.

(8)a. A person who establishes a new homestead as of January 1, 2009, or January 1 of any subsequent year and who has received a homestead exemption pursuant to Section 6 of this Article as of January 1 of either of the two years immediately preceding the establishment of the new homestead is entitled to have the new homestead assessed at less than just value. If this revision is approved in January of 2008, a person who establishes a new homestead as of January 1, 2008, is entitled to have the new homestead assessed at less than just value only if that person received a homestead exemption on January 1, 2007. The assessed value of the newly established homestead shall be determined as follows:

1. If the just value of the new homestead is greater than or equal to the just value of the prior homestead as of January 1 of the year in which the prior homestead was abandoned, the assessed value of the new homestead shall be the just value of the new homestead minus an amount equal to the lesser of $500,000 or the difference between the just value and the assessed value of the prior homestead as of January 1 of the year in which the prior homestead was abandoned. Thereafter, the homestead shall be assessed as provided in this subsection.
2. If the just value of the new homestead is less than the just value of the prior homestead as of January 1 of the year in which the prior homestead was abandoned, the assessed value of the new homestead shall be equal to the just value of the new homestead divided by the just value of the prior homestead and multiplied by the assessed value of the prior homestead. However, if the difference between the just value of the new homestead and the assessed value of the new homestead calculated pursuant to this sub-subparagraph is greater than $500,000, the assessed value of the new homestead shall be increased so that the difference between the just value and the assessed value equals $500,000. Thereafter, the homestead shall be assessed as provided in this subsection.

b. By general law and subject to conditions specified therein, the legislature shall provide for application of this paragraph to property owned by more than one person.

(e) The legislature may, by general law, for assessment purposes and subject to the provisions of this subsection, allow counties and municipalities to authorize by ordinance that historic property may be assessed solely on the basis of character or use. Such character or use assessment shall apply only to the jurisdiction adopting the ordinance. The requirements for eligible properties must be specified by general law.

(f) A county may, in the manner prescribed by general law, provide for a reduction in the assessed value of homestead property to the extent of any increase in the assessed value of that property which results from the construction or reconstruction of the property for the purpose of providing living quarters for one or more natural or adoptive grandparents or parents of the owner of the property or of the owner's spouse if at least one of the grandparents or parents for whom the living quarters are provided is 62 years of age or older. Such a reduction may not exceed the lesser of the following:

(1) The increase in assessed value resulting from construction or reconstruction of the property.
(2) Twenty percent of the total assessed value of the property as improved.

(g) For all levies other than school district levies, assessments of residential real property, as defined by general law, which contains nine units or fewer and which is not subject to the assessment limitations set forth in subsections (a) through (d) shall change only as provided in this subsection.

(1) Assessments subject to this subsection shall be changed annually on the date of assessment provided by law; but those changes in assessments shall not exceed ten percent (10%) of the assessment for the prior year.
(2) No assessment shall exceed just value.
(3) After a change of ownership or control, as defined by general law, including any change of ownership of a legal entity that owns the property, such property shall be assessed at just value as of the next assessment date. Thereafter, such property shall be assessed as provided in this subsection.
(4) Changes, additions, reductions, or improvements to such property shall be assessed as provided for by general law; however, after the adjustment for any change, addition, reduction, or improvement, the property shall be assessed as provided in this subsection.

(h) For all levies other than school district levies, assessments of real property that is not subject to the assessment limitations set forth in subsections (a) through (d) and (g) shall change only as provided in this subsection.

(1) Assessments subject to this subsection shall be changed annually on the date of assessment provided by law; but those changes in assessments shall not exceed ten percent (10%) of the assessment for the prior year.
(2) No assessment shall exceed just value.
(3) The legislature must provide that such property shall be assessed at just value as of the next assessment date after a qualifying improvement, as defined by general law, is made to such property. Thereafter, such property shall be assessed as provided in this subsection.
(4) The legislature may provide that such property shall be assessed at just value as of the next assessment date after a change of ownership or control, as defined by general law, including any change of ownership of the legal entity that owns the property. Thereafter, such property shall be assessed as provided in this subsection.
(5) Changes, additions, reductions, or improvements to such property shall be assessed as provided for by general law; however, after the adjustment for any change, addition, reduction, or improvement, the property shall be assessed as provided in this subsection.

(i) The legislature, by general law and subject to conditions specified therein, may prohibit the consideration of the following in the determination of the assessed value of real property:

(1) Any change or improvement to real property used for residential purposes made to improve the property's resistance to wind damage.
(2) The installation of a solar or renewable energy source device.

(j)
(1) The assessment of the following working waterfront properties shall be based upon the current use of the property:

a. Land used predominantly for commercial fishing purposes.
b. Land that is accessible to the public and used for vessel launches into waters that are navigable.
c. Marinas and drystacks that are open to the public.
d. Water-dependent marine manufacturing facilities, commercial fishing facilities, and marine vessel construction and repair facilities and their support activities.

(2) The assessment benefit provided by this subsection is subject to conditions and limitations and reasonable definitions as specified by the legislature by general law.

Section 5. Estate, Inheritance and Income Taxes

(a) Natural Persons.
No tax upon estates or inheritances or upon the income of natural persons who are residents or citizens of the state shall be levied by the state, or under its authority, in excess of the aggregate of amounts which may be allowed to be credited upon or deducted from any similar tax levied by the United States or any state.

(b) Others.
No tax upon the income of residents and citizens other than natural persons shall be levied by the state, or under its authority, in excess of 5% of net income, as defined by law, or at such greater rate as is authorized by a three-fifths (3/5) vote of the membership of each house of the legislature or as will provide for the state the maximum amount which may be allowed to be credited against income taxes levied by the United States and other states. There shall be exempt from taxation not less than five thousand dollars ($5,000) of the excess of net income subject to tax over the maximum amount allowed to be credited against income taxes levied by the United States and other states.

(c) Effective Date.
This section shall become effective immediately upon approval by the electors of Florida.

Section 6. Homestead Exemptions

(a) Every person who has the legal or equitable title to real estate and maintains thereon the permanent residence of the owner, or another legally or naturally dependent upon the owner, shall be exempt from taxation thereon, except assessments for special benefits, up to the assessed valuation of twenty-five thousand dollars and, for all levies other than school district levies, on the assessed valuation greater than fifty thousand dollars and up to seventy-five thousand dollars, upon establishment of right thereto in the manner prescribed by law. The real estate may be held by legal or equitable title, by the entireties, jointly, in common, as a condominium, or indirectly by stock ownership or membership representing the owner's or member's proprietary interest in a corporation owning a fee or a leasehold initially in excess of ninety-eight years. The exemption shall not apply with respect to any assessment roll until such roll is first determined to be in compliance with the provisions of section 4 by a state agency designated by general law. This exemption is repealed on the effective date of any amendment to this Article which provides for the assessment of homestead property at less than just value.
(b) Not more than one exemption shall be allowed any individual or family unit or with respect to any residential unit. No exemption shall exceed the value of the real estate assessable to the owner or, in case of ownership through stock or membership in a corporation, the value of the proportion which the interest in the corporation bears to the assessed value of the property.
(c) By general law and subject to conditions specified therein, the Legislature may provide to renters, who are permanent residents, ad valorem tax relief on all ad valorem tax levies. Such ad valorem tax relief shall be in the form and amount established by general law.

(d) The legislature may, by general law, allow counties or municipalities, for the purpose of their respective tax levies and subject to the provisions of general law, to grant either or both of the following additional homestead tax exemptions:

(1) An exemption not exceeding fifty thousand dollars to a person who has the legal or equitable title to real estate and maintains thereon the permanent residence of the owner, who has attained age sixty-five, and whose household income, as defined by general law, does not exceed twenty thousand dollars; or
(2) An exemption equal to the assessed value of the property to a person who has the legal or equitable title to real estate with a just value less than two hundred and fifty thousand dollars, as determined in the first tax year that the owner applies and is eligible for the exemption, and who has maintained thereon the permanent residence of the owner for not less than twenty-five years, who has attained age sixty-five, and whose household income does not exceed the income limitation prescribed in paragraph (1).

The general law must allow counties and municipalities to grant these additional exemptions, within the limits prescribed in this subsection, by ordinance adopted in the manner prescribed by general law, and must provide for the periodic adjustment of the income limitation prescribed in this subsection for changes in the cost of living.

(e) Each veteran who is age 65 or older who is partially or totally permanently disabled shall receive a discount from the amount of the ad valorem tax otherwise owed on homestead property the veteran owns and resides in if the disability was combat related and the veteran was honorably discharged upon separation from military service. The discount shall be in a percentage equal to the percentage of the veteran's permanent, service-connected disability as determined by the United States Department of Veterans Affairs. To qualify for the discount granted by this subsection, an applicant must submit to the county property appraiser, by March 1, an official letter from the United States Department of Veterans Affairs stating the percentage of the veteran's service-connected disability and such evidence that reasonably identifies the disability as combat related and a copy of the veteran's honorable discharge. If the property appraiser denies the request for a discount, the appraiser must notify the applicant in writing of the reasons for the denial, and the veteran may reapply. The Legislature may, by general law, waive the annual application requirement in subsequent years. This subsection is self-executing and does not require implementing legislation.

(f) By general law and subject to conditions and limitations specified therein, the Legislature may provide ad valorem tax relief equal to the total amount or a portion of the ad valorem tax otherwise owed on homestead property to:

(1) The surviving spouse of a veteran who died from service-connected causes while on active duty as a member of the United States Armed Forces.

(2) The surviving spouse of a first responder who died in the line of duty.

(3) A first responder who is totally and permanently disabled as a result of an injury or injuries sustained in the line of duty. Causal connection between a disability and service in the line of duty shall not be presumed but must be determined as provided by general law. For purposes of this paragraph, the term "disability" does not include a chronic condition or chronic disease, unless the injury sustained in the line of duty was the sole cause of the chronic condition or chronic disease.

As used in this subsection and as further defined by general law, the term "first responder" means a law enforcement officer, a correctional officer, a firefighter, an emergency medical technician, or a paramedic, and the term "in the line of duty" means arising out of and in the actual performance of duty required by employment as a first responder.

Section 7. Allocation of Pari-Mutuel Taxes

Taxes upon the operation of pari-mutuel pools may be preempted to the state or allocated in whole or in part to the counties. When allocated to the counties, the distribution shall be in equal amounts to the several counties.

Section 8. Aid to Local Governments

State funds may be appropriated to the several counties, school districts, municipalities or special districts upon such conditions as may be provided by general law. These conditions may include the use of relative ad valorem assessment levels determined by a state agency designated by general law.

Section 9. Local Taxes

(a) Counties, school districts, and municipalities shall, and special districts may, be authorized by law to levy ad valorem taxes and may be authorized by general law to levy other taxes, for their respective purposes, except ad valorem taxes on intangible personal property and taxes prohibited by this constitution.

(b) Ad valorem taxes, exclusive of taxes levied for the payment of bonds and taxes levied for periods not longer than two years when authorized by vote of the electors who are the owners of freeholds therein not wholly exempt from taxation, shall not be levied in excess of the following millages upon the assessed value of real estate and tangible personal property: for all county purposes, ten mills; for all municipal purposes, ten mills; for all school purposes, ten mills; for water management purposes for the northwest portion of the state lying west of the line between ranges two and three east, 0.05 mill; for water management purposes for the remaining portions of the state, 1.0 mill; and for all other special districts a millage authorized by law approved by vote of the electors who are owners of freeholds therein not wholly exempt from taxation. A county furnishing municipal services may, to the extent authorized by law, levy additional taxes within the limits fixed for municipal purposes.

Section 10. Pledging Credit
Neither the state nor any county, school district, municipality, special district, or agency of any of them, shall become a joint owner with, or stockholder of, or give, lend or use its taxing power or credit to aid any corporation, association, partnership or person; but this shall not prohibit laws authorizing:

(a) the investment of public trust funds;
(b) the investment of other public funds in obligations of, or insured by, the United States or any of its instrumentalities;
(c) the issuance and sale by any county, municipality, special district or other local governmental body of (1) revenue bonds to finance or refinance the cost of capital projects for airports or port facilities, or (2) revenue bonds to finance or refinance the cost of capital projects for industrial or manufacturing plants to the extent that the interest thereon is exempt from income taxes under the then existing laws of the United States, when, in either case, the revenue bonds are payable solely from revenue derived from the sale, operation or leasing of the projects. If any project so financed, or any part thereof, is occupied or operated by any private corporation, association, partnership or person pursuant to contract or lease with the issuing body, the property interest created by such contract or lease shall be subject to taxation to the same extent as other privately owned property.
(d) a municipality, county, special district, or agency of any of them, being a joint owner of, giving, or lending or using its taxing power or credit for the joint ownership, construction and operation of electrical energy generating or transmission facilities with any corporation, association, partnership or person.

Section 11. State Bonds; Revenue Bonds

(a) State bonds pledging the full faith and credit of the state may be issued only to finance or refinance the cost of state fixed capital outlay projects authorized by law, and purposes incidental thereto, upon approval by a vote of the electors; provided state bonds issued pursuant to this subsection may be refunded without a vote of the electors at a lower net average interest cost rate. The total outstanding principal of state bonds issued pursuant to this subsection shall never exceed fifty percent of the total tax revenues of the state for the two preceding fiscal years, excluding any tax revenues held in trust under the provisions of this constitution.

(b) Moneys sufficient to pay debt service on state bonds as the same becomes due shall be appropriated by law.

(c) Any state bonds pledging the full faith and credit of the state issued under this section or any other section of this constitution may be combined for the purposes of sale.

(d) Revenue bonds may be issued by the state or its agencies without a vote of the electors to finance or refinance the cost of state fixed capital outlay projects authorized by law, and purposes incidental thereto, and shall be payable solely from funds derived directly from sources other than state tax revenues.

(e) Bonds pledging all or part of a dedicated state tax revenue may be issued by the state in the manner provided by general law to finance or refinance the acquisition and improvement of land, water areas, and related property interests and resources for the purposes of conservation, outdoor recreation, water resource development, restoration of natural systems, and historic preservation.

(f) Each project, building, or facility to be financed or refinanced with revenue bonds issued under this section shall first be approved by the Legislature by an act relating to appropriations or by general law.

Section 12. Local Bonds

Counties, school districts, municipalities, special districts and local governmental bodies with taxing powers may issue bonds, certificates of indebtedness or any form of tax anticipation certificates, payable from ad valorem taxation and maturing more than twelve months after issuance only:

(a) to finance or refinance capital projects authorized by law and only when approved by vote of the electors who are owners of freeholds therein not wholly exempt from taxation; or

(b) to refund outstanding bonds and interest and redemption premium thereon at a lower net average interest cost rate.

Section 13. Relief from Illegal Taxes

Until payment of all taxes which have been legally assessed upon the property of the same owner, no court shall grant relief from the payment of any tax that may be illegal or illegally assessed.

Section 14. Bonds for Pollution Control and Abatement and other Water Facilities

(a) When authorized by law, state bonds pledging the full faith and credit of the state may be issued without an election to finance the construction of air and water pollution control and abatement and solid waste disposal facilities and other water facilities authorized by general law (herein referred to as "facilities") to be operated by any municipality, county, district or authority, or any agency thereof (herein referred to as "local governmental agencies"), or by any agency of the State of Florida. Such bonds shall be secured by a pledge of and shall be payable primarily from all or any part of revenues to be derived from operation of such facilities, special assessments, rentals to be received under lease-purchase agreements herein provided for, any other revenues that may be legally available for such purpose, including revenues from other facilities, or any combination thereof (herein collectively referred to as "pledged revenues"), and shall be additionally secured by the full faith and credit of the State of Florida.

(b) No such bonds shall be issued unless a state fiscal agency, created by law, has made a determination that in no state fiscal year will the debt service requirements of the bonds proposed to be issued and all other bonds secured by the pledged revenues exceed seventy-five per cent of the pledged revenues.

(c) The state may lease any of such facilities to any local governmental agency, under lease-purchase agreements for such periods and under such other terms and conditions as may be mutually agreed upon. The local governmental agencies may pledge the revenues derived from such leased facilities or any other available funds for the payment of rentals thereunder; and, in addition, the full faith and credit and taxing power of such local governmental agencies may be pledged for the payment of such rentals without any election of freeholder electors or qualified electors.

(d) The state may also issue such bonds for the purpose of loaning money to local governmental agencies, for the construction of such facilities to be owned or operated by any of such local governmental agencies. Such loans shall bear interest at not more than one-half of one per cent per annum greater than the last preceding issue of state bonds pursuant to this section, shall be secured by the pledged revenues, and may be additionally secured by the full faith and credit of the local governmental agencies.

(e) The total outstanding principal of state bonds issued pursuant to this section 14 shall never exceed fifty per cent of the total tax revenues of the state for the two preceding fiscal years.

Section 15. Revenue Bonds for Scholarship Loans

(a) When authorized by law, revenue bonds may be issued to establish a fund to make loans to students determined eligible as prescribed by law and who have been admitted to attend any public or private institutions of higher learning, junior colleges, health related training institutions, or vocational training centers, which are recognized or accredited under terms and conditions prescribed by law. Revenue bonds issued pursuant to this section shall be secured by a pledge of and shall be payable primarily from payments of interest, principal, and handling charges to such fund from the recipients of the loans and, if authorized by law, may be additionally secured by student fees and by any other moneys in such fund. There shall be established from the proceeds of each issue of revenue bonds a reserve account in an amount equal to and sufficient to pay the greatest amount of principal, interest, and handling charges to become due on such issue in any ensuing state fiscal year.

(b) Interest moneys in the fund established pursuant to this section, not required in any fiscal year for payment of debt service on then outstanding revenue bonds or for maintenance of the reserve account, may be used for educational loans to students determined to be eligible therefor in the manner provided by law, or for such other related purposes as may be provided by law.

Section 16. Bonds for Housing and Related Facilities

(a) When authorized by law, revenue bonds may be issued without an election to finance or refinance housing and related facilities in Florida, herein referred to as "facilities."
(b) The bonds shall be secured by a pledge of and shall be payable primarily from all or any part of revenues to be derived from the financing, operation or sale of such facilities, mortgage or loan payments, and any other revenues or assets that may be legally available for such purposes derived from sources other than ad valorem taxation, including revenues from other facilities, or any combination thereof, herein collectively referred to as "pledged revenues," provided that in no event shall the full faith and credit of the state be pledged to secure such revenue bonds.
(c) No bonds shall be issued unless a state fiscal agency, created by law, has made a determination that in no state fiscal year will the debt service requirements of the bonds proposed to be issued and all other bonds secured by the same pledged revenues exceed the pledged revenues available for payment of such debt service requirements, as defined by law.

Section 17. Bonds for Acquiring Transportation Right-Of-Way or for Constructing Bridges

(a) When authorized by law, state bonds pledging the full faith and credit of the state may be issued, without a vote of the electors, to finance or refinance the cost of acquiring real property or the rights to real property for state roads as defined by law, or to finance or refinance the cost of state bridge construction, and purposes incidental to such property acquisition or state bridge construction.

(b) Bonds issued under this section shall be secured by a pledge of and shall be payable primarily from motor fuel or special fuel taxes, except those defined in Section 9(c) of Article XII, as provided by law, and shall additionally be secured by the full faith and credit of the state.

(c) No bonds shall be issued under this section unless a state fiscal agency, created by law, has made a determination that in no state fiscal year will the debt service requirements of the bonds proposed to be issued and all other bonds secured by the same pledged revenues exceed ninety percent of the pledged revenues available for payment of such debt service requirements, as defined by law. For the purposes of this subsection, the term "pledged revenues" means all revenues pledged to the payment of debt service, excluding any pledge of the full faith and credit of the state.

Section 18. Laws Requiring Counties or Municipalities to Spend Funds or Limiting Their Ability to Raise Revenue or Receive State Tax Revenue

(a) No county or municipality shall be bound by any general law requiring such county or municipality to spend funds or to take an action requiring the expenditure of funds unless the legislature has determined that such law fulfills an important state interest and unless: funds have been appropriated that have been estimated at the time of enactment to be sufficient to fund such expenditure; the legislature authorizes or has authorized a county or municipality to enact a funding source not available for such county or municipality on February 1, 1989, that can be used to generate the amount of funds estimated to be sufficient to fund such expenditure by a simple majority vote of the governing body of such county or municipality; the law requiring such expenditure is approved by two-thirds of the membership in each house of the legislature; the expenditure is required to comply with a law that applies to all persons similarly situated, including the state and local governments; or the law is either required to comply with a federal requirement or required for eligibility for a federal entitlement, which federal requirement specifically contemplates actions by counties or municipalities for compliance.

(b) Except upon approval of each house of the legislature by two-thirds of the membership, the legislature may not enact, amend, or repeal any general law if the anticipated effect of doing so would be to reduce the authority that municipalities or counties have to raise revenues in the aggregate, as such authority exists on February 1, 1989.

(c) Except upon approval of each house of the legislature by two-thirds of the membership, the legislature may not enact, amend, or repeal any general law if the anticipated effect of doing so would be to reduce the percentage of a state tax shared with counties and municipalities as an aggregate on February 1, 1989. The provisions of this subsection shall not apply to enhancements enacted after February 1, 1989, to state tax sources, or during a fiscal emergency declared in a written joint proclamation issued by the president of the senate and the speaker of the house of representatives, or where the legislature provides additional state-shared revenues which are anticipated to be sufficient to replace the anticipated aggregate loss of state-shared revenues resulting from the reduction of the percentage of the state tax shared with counties and municipalities, which source of replacement revenues shall be subject to the same requirements for repeal or modification as provided herein for a state-shared tax source existing on February 1, 1989.

(d) Laws adopted to require funding of pension benefits existing on the effective date of this section, criminal laws, election laws, the general appropriations act, special appropriations acts, laws reauthorizing but not expanding then-existing statutory authority, laws having insignificant fiscal impact, and laws creating, modifying, or repealing noncriminal infractions, are exempt from the requirements of this section.

(e) The legislature may enact laws to assist in the implementation and enforcement of this section.

ARTICLE VIII: LOCAL GOVERNMENT

Section 1. Counties

(a) Political Subdivisions.
The state shall be divided by law into political subdivisions called counties. Counties may be created, abolished or changed by law, with provision for payment or apportionment of the public debt.

(b) County Funds.
The care, custody and method of disbursing county funds shall be provided by general law.

(c) Government.
Pursuant to general or special law, a county government may be established by charter which shall be adopted, amended or repealed only upon vote of the electors of the county in a special election called for that purpose.

(d) County Officers.
There shall be elected by the electors of each county, for terms of four years, a sheriff, a tax collector, a property appraiser, a supervisor of elections, and a clerk of the circuit court; except, when provided by county charter or special law approved by vote of the electors of the county, any county officer may be chosen in another manner therein specified, or any county office may be abolished when all the duties of the office prescribed by general law are transferred to another office. When not otherwise provided by county charter or special law approved by vote of the electors, the clerk of the circuit court shall be ex officio clerk of the board of county commissioners, auditor, recorder and custodian of all county funds.

(e) Commissioners.
Except when otherwise provided by county charter, the governing body of each county shall be a board of county commissioners composed of five or seven members serving staggered terms of four years. After each decennial census the board of county

commissioners shall divide the county into districts of contiguous territory as nearly equal in population as practicable. One commissioner residing in each district shall be elected as provided by law.

(f) Non-Charter Government.
Counties not operating under county charters shall have such power of self-government as is provided by general or special law. The board of county commissioners of a county not operating under a charter may enact, in a manner prescribed by general law, county ordinances not inconsistent with general or special law, but an ordinance in conflict with a municipal ordinance shall not be effective within the municipality to the extent of such conflict.

(g) Charter Government.
Counties operating under county charters shall have all powers of local self-government not inconsistent with general law, or with special law approved by vote of the electors. The governing body of a county operating under a charter may enact county ordinances not inconsistent with general law. The charter shall provide which shall prevail in the event of conflict between county and municipal ordinances.

(h) Taxes; Limitation.
Property situate within municipalities shall not be subject to taxation for services rendered by the county exclusively for the benefit of the property or residents in unincorporated areas.

(i) County Ordinances.
Each county ordinance shall be filed with the custodian of state records and shall become effective at such time thereafter as is provided by general law.

(j) Violation Of Ordinances.
Persons violating county ordinances shall be prosecuted and punished as provided by law.

(k) County Seat.
In every county there shall be a county seat at which shall be located the principal offices and permanent records of all county officers. The county seat may not be moved except as provided by general law. Branch offices for the conduct of county business may be established elsewhere in the county by resolution of the governing body of the county in the manner prescribed by law. No instrument shall be deemed recorded until filed at the county seat, or a branch office designated by the governing body of the county for the recording of instruments, according to law.

Section 2. Municipalities

(a) Establishment.
Municipalities may be established or abolished and their charters amended pursuant to general or special law. When any municipality is abolished, provision shall be made for the protection of its creditors.

(b) Powers.
Municipalities shall have governmental, corporate and proprietary powers to enable them to conduct municipal government, perform municipal functions and render municipal services, and may exercise any power for municipal purposes except as otherwise provided by law. Each municipal legislative body shall be elective.

(c) Annexation.
Municipal annexation of unincorporated territory, merger of municipalities, and exercise of extra-territorial powers by municipalities shall be as provided by general or special law.

Section 3. Consolidation
The government of a county and the government of one or more municipalities located therein may be consolidated into a single government which may exercise any and all powers of the county and the several municipalities. The consolidation plan may be proposed only by special law, which shall become effective if

approved by vote of the electors of the county, or of the county and municipalities affected, as may be provided in the plan. Consolidation shall not extend the territorial scope of taxation for the payment of pre-existing debt except to areas whose residents receive a benefit from the facility or service for which the indebtedness was incurred.

Section 4. Transfer of Powers

By law or by resolution of the governing bodies of each of the governments affected, any function or power of a county, municipality or special district may be transferred to or contracted to be performed by another county, municipality or special district, after approval by vote of the electors of the transferor and approval by vote of the electors of the transferee, or as otherwise provided by law.

Section 5. Local Option

(a) Local option on the legality or prohibition of the sale of intoxicating liquors, wines or beers shall be preserved to each county. The status of a county with respect thereto shall be changed only by vote of the electors in a special election called upon the petition of twenty-five per cent of the electors of the county, and not sooner than two years after an earlier election on the same question. Where legal, the sale of intoxicating liquors, wines and beers shall be regulated by law.

(b) Each county shall have the authority to require a criminal history records check and a 3 to 5-day waiting period, excluding weekends and legal holidays, in connection with the sale of any firearm occurring within such county. For purposes of this subsection, the term "sale" means the transfer of money or other valuable consideration for any firearm when any part of the transaction is conducted on property to which the public has the right of access. Holders of a concealed weapons permit as prescribed by general law shall not be subject to the provisions of this subsection when purchasing a firearm.

Section 6. Schedule to Article VIII

(a) This article shall replace all of Article VIII of the Constitution of 1885, as amended, except those sections expressly retained and made a part of this article by reference.

(b) Counties; County Seats; Municipalities; Districts.
The status of the following items as they exist on the date this article becomes effective is recognized and shall be continued until changed in accordance with law: the counties of the state; their status with respect to the legality of the sale of intoxicating liquors, wines and beers; the method of selection of county officers; the performance of municipal functions by county officers; the county seats; and the municipalities and special districts of the state, their powers, jurisdiction and government.

(c) Officers to Continue in Office.
Every person holding office when this article becomes effective shall continue in office for the remainder of the term if that office is not abolished. If the office is abolished the incumbent shall be paid adequate compensation, to be fixed by law, for the loss of emoluments for the remainder of the term.

(d) Ordinances.
Local laws relating only to unincorporated areas of a county on the effective date of this article may be amended or repealed by county ordinance.

(e) Consolidation and Home Rule.
Article VIII, Sections 19, 210, 311 and 424, of the Constitution of 1885, as amended, shall remain in full force and effect as to each county affected, as if this article had not been adopted, until that county shall expressly adopt a charter or home rule plan pursuant to this article. All provisions of the Metropolitan Dade County Home Rule Charter, heretofore or hereafter adopted by the electors of Dade County pursuant to Article VIII, Section 11, of the Constitution of 1885, as amended, shall be valid, and any amendments to such charter shall be valid; provided that the said provisions of such charter and the said amendments thereto are authorized under said Article VIII, Section 11, of the Constitution of 1885, as amended.

(f) Dade County; Powers Conferred upon Municipalities.
To the extent not inconsistent with the powers of existing municipalities or general law, the Metropolitan Government of Dade County may exercise all the powers conferred now or hereafter by general law upon municipalities.

(g) Deletion of Obsolete Schedule Items.
The legislature shall have power, by joint resolution, to delete from this article any subsection of this Section 6, including this subsection, when all events to which the subsection to be deleted is or could become applicable have occurred. A legislative determination of fact made as a basis for application of this subsection shall be subject to judicial review.

Section 9. Legislative Power Over City of Jacksonville and Duval County

The Legislature shall have power to establish, alter or abolish, a Municipal corporation to be known as the City of Jacksonville, extending territorially throughout the present limits of Duval County, in the place of any or all county, district, municipal and local governments, boards, bodies and officers, constitutional or statutory, legislative, executive, judicial, or administrative, and shall prescribe the jurisdiction, powers, duties and functions of such municipal corporation, its legislative, executive, judicial and administrative departments and its boards, bodies and officers; to divide the territory included in such municipality into subordinate districts, and to prescribe a just and reasonable system of taxation for such municipality and districts; and to fix the liability of such municipality and districts. Bonded and other indebtedness, existing at the time of the establishment of such municipality, shall be enforceable only against property theretofore taxable therefor. The Legislature shall, from time to time, determine what portion of said municipality is a rural area, and a homestead in such rural area shall not be limited as if in a city or town. Such municipality may exercise all the powers of a municipal corporation and shall also be recognized as one of the legal political divisions of the State with the duties and obligations of a county and shall be entitled to all the powers, rights and privileges, including representation in the State

Legislature, which would accrue to it if it were a county. All property of Duval County and of the municipalities in said county shall vest in such municipal corporation when established as herein provided. The offices of Clerk of the Circuit Court and Sheriff shall not be abolished but the Legislature may prescribe the time when, and the method by which, such offices shall be filled and the compensation to be paid to such officers and may vest in them additional powers and duties. No county office shall be abolished or consolidated with another office without making provision for the performance of all State duties now or hereafter prescribed by law to be performed by such county officer. Nothing contained herein shall affect Section 20 of Article III of the Constitution of the State of Florida, except as to such provisions therein as relate to regulating the jurisdiction and duties of any class of officers, to summoning and impanelling grand and petit jurors, to assessing and collecting taxes for county purposes and to regulating the fees and compensation of county officers. No law authorizing the establishing or abolishing of such Municipal corporation pursuant to this Section, shall become operative or effective until approved by a majority of the qualified electors participating in an election held in said County, but so long as such Municipal corporation exists under this Section the Legislature may amend or extend the law authorizing the same without referendum to the qualified voters unless the Legislative act providing for such amendment or extension shall provide for such referendum.

Section 10. Legislative Power Over City of Key West and Monroe County

The Legislature shall have power to establish, alter or abolish, a Municipal corporation to be known as the City of Key West, extending territorially throughout the present limits of Monroe County, in the place of any or all county, district, municipal and local governments, boards, bodies and officers, constitutional or statutory, legislative, executive, judicial, or administrative, and shall prescribe the jurisdiction, powers, duties and functions of such municipal corporation, its legislative, executive, judicial and administrative departments and its boards, bodies and officers;

to divide the territory included in such municipality into subordinate districts, and to prescribe a just and reasonable system of taxation for such municipality and districts; and to fix the liability of such municipality and districts. Bonded and other indebtedness, existing at the time of the establishment of such municipality, shall be enforceable only against property theretofore taxable therefor. The Legislature shall, from time to time, determine what portion of said municipality is a rural area, and a homestead in such rural area shall not be limited as if in a city or town. Such municipality may exercise all the powers of a municipal corporation and shall also be recognized as one of the legal political divisions of the State with the duties and obligations of a county and shall be entitled to all the powers, rights and privileges, including representation in the State Legislature, which would accrue to it if it were a county. All property of Monroe County and of the municipality in said county shall vest in such municipal corporation when established as herein provided. The offices of Clerk of the Circuit Court and Sheriff shall not be abolished but the Legislature may prescribe the time when, and the method by which, such offices shall be filled and the compensation to be paid to such officers and may vest in them additional powers and duties. No county office shall be abolished or consolidated with another office without making provision for the performance of all State duties now or hereafter prescribed by law to be performed by such county officer. Nothing contained herein shall affect Section 20 of Article III of the Constitution of the State of Florida, except as to such provisions therein as relate to regulating the jurisdiction and duties of any class of officers, to summoning and impanelling grand and petit juries, to assessing and collecting taxes for county purposes and to regulating the fees and compensation of county officers. No law authorizing the establishing or abolishing of such Municipal corporation pursuant to this Section shall become operative or effective until approved by a majority of the qualified electors participating in an election held in said County, but so long as such Municipal corporation exists under this Section the Legislature may amend or extend the law authorizing the same without referendum to the qualified voters unless the

Legislative Act providing for such amendment or extension shall provide for such referendum.

Section 11. Dade County, Home Rule Charter

(1) The electors of Dade County, Florida, are granted power to adopt, revise, and amend from time to time a home rule charter of government for Dade County, Florida, under which the Board of County Commissioners of Dade County shall be the governing body. This charter:

(a) Shall fix the boundaries of each county commission district, provide a method for changing them from time to time, and fix the number, terms and compensation of the commissioners, and their method of election.
(b) May grant full power and authority to the Board of County Commissioners of Dade County to pass ordinances relating to the affairs, property and government of Dade County and provide suitable penalties for the violation thereof; to levy and collect such taxes as may be authorized by general law and no other taxes, and to do everything necessary to carry on a central metropolitan government in Dade County.
(c) May change the boundaries of, merge, consolidate, and abolish and may provide a method for changing the boundaries of, merging, consolidating and abolishing from time to time all municipal corporations, county or district governments, special taxing districts, authorities, boards, or other governmental units whose jurisdiction lies wholly within Dade County, whether such governmental units are created by the Constitution or the Legislature or otherwise, except the Dade County Board of County Commissioners as it may be provided for from time to time by this home rule charter and the Board of Public Instruction of Dade County.
(d) May provide a method by which any and all of the functions or powers of any municipal corporation or other governmental unit in Dade County may be transferred to the Board of County Commissioners of Dade County.

(e) May provide a method for establishing new municipal corporations, special taxing districts, and other governmental units in Dade County from time to time and provide for their government and prescribe their jurisdiction and powers.
(f) May abolish and may provide a method for abolishing from time to time all offices provided for by Article VIII, Section 6, of the Constitution or by the Legislature, except the Superintendent of Public Instruction and may provide for the consolidation and transfer of the functions of such offices, provided, however, that there shall be no power to abolish or impair the jurisdiction of the Circuit Court or to abolish any other court provided for by this Constitution or by general law, or the judges or clerks thereof although such charter may create new courts and judges and clerks thereof with jurisdiction to try all offenses against ordinances passed by the Board of County Commissioners of Dade County and none of the other courts provided for by this Constitution or by general law shall have original jurisdiction to try such offenses, although the charter may confer appellate jurisdiction on such courts, and provided further that if said home rule charter shall abolish any county office or offices as authorized herein, that said charter shall contain adequate provision for the carrying on of all functions of said office or offices as are now or may hereafter be prescribed by general law.
(g) Shall provide a method by which each municipal corporation in Dade County shall have the power to make, amend or repeal its own charter. Upon adoption of this home rule charter by the electors this method shall be exclusive and the Legislature shall have no power to amend or repeal the charter of any municipal corporation in Dade County.
(h) May change the name of Dade County.
(i) Shall provide a method for the recall of any commissioner and a method for initiative and referendum, including the initiation of and referendum on ordinances and the amendment or revision of the home rule charter, provided, however, that the power of the Governor and Senate relating to the suspension and removal of officers provided for in this Constitution shall not be impaired, but shall extend to all officers provided for in said home rule

charter.

(2) Provision shall be made for the protection of the creditors of any governmental unit which is merged, consolidated, or abolished or whose boundaries are changed or functions or powers transferred.

(3) This home rule charter shall be prepared by a Metropolitan Charter Board created by the Legislature and shall be presented to the electors of Dade County for ratification or rejection in the manner provided by the Legislature. Until a home rule charter is adopted the Legislature may from time to time create additional Charter Boards to prepare charters to be presented to the electors of Dade County for ratification or rejection in the manner provided by the Legislature. Such Charter, once adopted by the electors, may be amended only by the electors of Dade County and this charter shall provide a method for submitting future charter revisions and amendments to the electors of Dade County.

(4) The County Commission shall continue to receive its pro rata share of all revenues payable by the state from whatever source to the several counties and the state of Florida shall pay to the Commission all revenues which would have been paid to any municipality in Dade County which may be abolished by or in the method provided by this home rule charter; provided, however, the Commission shall reimburse the comptroller of Florida for the expense incurred if any, in the keeping of separate records to determine the amounts of money which would have been payable to any such municipality.

(5) Nothing in this section shall limit or restrict the power of the Legislature to enact general laws which shall relate to Dade County and any other one or more counties in the state of Florida or to any municipality in Dade County and any other one or more municipalities of the State of Florida, and the home rule charter provided for herein shall not conflict with any provision of this Constitution nor of any applicable general laws now applying to Dade County and any other one or more counties of the State of Florida except as expressly authorized in this section nor shall any ordinance enacted in pursuance to said home rule charter conflict with this Constitution or any such applicable general law except as expressly authorized herein, nor shall the charter of any municipality in Dade County conflict with this Constitution or any such applicable general law except as expressly authorized herein, provided however that said charter and said ordinances enacted in pursuance thereof may conflict with, modify or nullify any existing local, special or general law applicable only to Dade County.

(6) Nothing in this section shall be construed to limit or restrict the power of the Legislature to enact general laws which shall relate to Dade County and any other one or more counties of the state of Florida or to any municipality in Dade County and any other one or more municipalities of the State of Florida relating to county or municipal affairs and all such general laws shall apply to Dade County and to all municipalities therein to the same extent as if this section had not been adopted and such general laws shall supersede any part or portion of the home rule charter provided for herein in conflict therewith and shall supersede any provision of any ordinance enacted pursuant to said charter and in conflict therewith, and shall supersede any provision of any charter of any municipality in Dade County in conflict therewith.

(7) Nothing in this section shall be construed to limit or restrict the power and jurisdiction of the Railroad and Public Utilities Commission or of any other state agency, bureau or commission now or hereafter provided for in this Constitution or by general law and said state agencies, bureaus and commissions shall have the same powers in Dade County as shall be conferred upon them in regard to other counties.

(8) If any section, subsection, sentence, clause or provisions of this section is held invalid as violative of the provisions of Section 1 Article XVII of this Constitution the remainder of this section shall not be affected by such invalidity.

(9) It is declared to be the intent of the Legislature and of the electors of the State of Florida to provide by this section home rule for the people of Dade County in local affairs and this section shall be liberally construed to carry out such purpose, and it is further declared to be the intent of the Legislature and of the electors of the State of Florida that the provisions of this Constitution and general laws which shall relate to Dade County and any other one or more counties of the State of Florida or to any municipality in Dade County and any other one or more municipalities of the State of Florida enacted pursuant thereto by the Legislature shall be the supreme law in Dade County, Florida, except as expressly provided herein and this section shall be strictly construed to maintain such supremacy of this Constitution and of the Legislature in the enactment of general laws pursuant to this Constitution.

Section 24. Hillsborough County, Home Rule Charter

(1) The electors of Hillsborough county are hereby granted the power to adopt a charter for a government which shall exercise any and all powers for county and municipal purposes which this constitution or the legislature, by general, special or local law, has conferred upon Hillsborough county or any municipality therein. Such government shall exercise these powers by the enactment of ordinances which relate to government of Hillsborough county and provide suitable penalties for the violation thereof. Such government shall have no power to create or abolish any municipality, except as otherwise provided herein.
(2) The method and manner by which the electors of Hillsborough county shall exercise this power shall be set forth in a charter for the government of Hillsborough county which charter shall be presented to said electors by any charter commission established by the legislature. The legislature may provide for the continuing existence of any charter commission or may establish a charter commission or commissions subsequent to any initial commission without regard to any election or elections held upon any charter or charters theretofore presented. A charter shall become effective only upon ratification by a majority of the electors of Hillsborough county voting in a general or special election as provided by law.

(3) The number, qualifications, terms of office and method of filling vacancies in the membership of any charter commission established pursuant to this section and the powers, functions and duties of any such commission shall be provided by law.

(4) A charter prepared by any commission established pursuant to this section shall provide that:

(a) The governments of the city of Tampa and the county of Hillsborough shall be consolidated, and the structure of the new local government shall include:

1. An executive branch, the chief officer of which shall be responsible for the administration of government.
2. An elected legislative branch, the election to membership, powers and duties of which shall be as provided by the charter.
3. A judicial branch, which shall only have jurisdiction in the enforcement of ordinances enacted by the legislative branch created by this section.

(b) Should the electors of the municipalities of Plant City or Temple Terrace wish to consolidate their governments with the government hereinabove created, they may do so by majority vote of the electors of said municipality voting in an election upon said issue.

(c) The creditors of any governmental unit consolidated or abolished under this section shall be protected. Bonded or other indebtedness existing at the effective date of any government established hereunder shall be enforceable only against the real and personal property theretofore taxable for such purposes.

(d) Such other provisions as might be required by law.

(5) The provisions of such charter and ordinances enacted pursuant thereto shall not conflict with any provision of this constitution nor with general, special or local laws now or hereafter applying to Hillsborough county.

(6) The government established hereunder shall be recognized as a county, that is one of the legal political subdivisions of the state with the powers, rights, privileges, duties and obligations of a county, and may also exercise all the powers of a municipality. Said government shall have the right to sue and be sued.

(7) Any government established hereunder shall be entitled to receive from the state of Florida or from the United States or from any other agency, public or private, funds and revenues to which a county is, or may hereafter be entitled, and also all funds and revenues to which an incorporated municipality is or may hereafter be entitled, and to receive the same without diminution or loss by reason of any such government as may be established. Nothing herein contained shall preclude such government as may be established hereunder from receiving all funds and revenues from whatever source now received, or hereinafter received provided by law.

(8) The board of county commissioners of Hillsborough county shall be abolished when the functions, duties, powers and responsibilities of said board shall be transferred in the manner to be provided by the charter to the government established pursuant to this section. No other office provided for by this constitution shall be abolished by or pursuant to this section.

(9) This section shall not restrict or limit the legislature in the enactment of general, special or local laws as otherwise provided in this constitution.

ARTICLE IX: EDUCATION

Section 1. Public Education

(a) The education of children is a fundamental value of the people of the State of Florida. It is, therefore, a paramount duty of the state to make adequate provision for the education of all children residing within its borders. Adequate provision shall be made by law for a uniform, efficient, safe, secure, and high quality system of free public schools that allows students to obtain a high quality education and for the establishment, maintenance, and operation of institutions of higher learning and other public education programs that the needs of the people may require. To assure that children attending public schools obtain a high quality education, the legislature shall make adequate provision to ensure that, by the beginning of the 2010 school year, there are a sufficient number of classrooms so that:

(1) The maximum number of students who are assigned to each teacher who is teaching in public school classrooms for prekindergarten through grade 3 does not exceed 18 students;
(2) The maximum number of students who are assigned to each teacher who is teaching in public school classrooms for grades 4 through 8 does not exceed 22 students; and
(3) The maximum number of students who are assigned to each teacher who is teaching in public school classrooms for grades 9 through 12 does not exceed 25 students.
The class size requirements of this subsection do not apply to extracurricular classes. Payment of the costs associated with reducing class size to meet these requirements is the responsibility of the state and not of local schools districts. Beginning with the 2003-2004 fiscal year, the legislature shall provide sufficient funds to reduce the average number of students in each classroom by at least two students per year until the maximum number of students per classroom does not exceed the requirements of this subsection.

(b) Every four-year old child in Florida shall be provided by the State a high quality pre-kindergarten learning opportunity in the form of an early childhood development and education program which shall be voluntary, high quality, free, and delivered according to professionally accepted standards. An early childhood development and education program means an organized program designed to address and enhance each child's ability to make age appropriate progress in an appropriate range of settings in the development of language and cognitive capabilities and emotional, social, regulatory and moral capacities through education in basic skills and such other skills as the Legislature may determine to be appropriate.
(c) The early childhood education and development programs provided by reason of subparagraph (b) shall be implemented no later than the beginning of the 2005 school year through funds generated in addition to those used for existing education, health, and development programs. Existing education, health, and development programs are those funded by the State as of January 1, 2002 that provided for child or adult education, health care, or development.

Section 2. State Board Of Education
The state board of education shall be a body corporate and have such supervision of the system of free public education as is provided by law. The state board of education shall consist of seven members appointed by the governor to staggered 4-year terms, subject to confirmation by the senate. The state board of education shall appoint the commissioner of education.

Section 3. Terms of Appointive Board Members
Members of any appointive board dealing with education may serve terms in excess of four years as provided by law.

Section 4. School Districts; School Boards

(a) Each county shall constitute a school district; provided, two or more contiguous counties, upon vote of the electors of each county pursuant to law, may be combined into one school district. In each school district there shall be a school board composed of five or more members chosen by vote of the electors in a nonpartisan election for appropriately staggered terms of four years, as provided by law.

(b) The school board shall operate, control and supervise all free public schools within the school district and determine the rate of school district taxes within the limits prescribed herein. Two or more school districts may operate and finance joint educational programs.

Section 5. Superintendent of Schools

In each school district there shall be a superintendent of schools who shall be elected at the general election in each year the number of which is a multiple of four for a term of four years; or, when provided by resolution of the district school board, or by special law, approved by vote of the electors, the district school superintendent in any school district shall be employed by the district school board as provided by general law. The resolution or special law may be rescinded or repealed by either procedure after four years.

Section 6. State School Fund

The income derived from the state school fund shall, and the principal of the fund may, be appropriated, but only to the support and maintenance of free public schools.

Section 7. State University System

(a) Purposes.
In order to achieve excellence through teaching students, advancing research and providing public service for the benefit of Florida's citizens, their communities and economies, the people hereby establish a system of governance for the state university system of Florida.

(b) State University System.
There shall be a single state university system comprised of all public universities. A board of trustees shall administer each public university and a board of governors shall govern the state university system.

(c) Local Boards Of Trustees.
Each local constituent university shall be administered by a board of trustees consisting of thirteen members dedicated to the purposes of the state university system. The board of governors shall establish the powers and duties of the boards of trustees. Each board of trustees shall consist of six citizen members appointed by the governor and five citizen members appointed by the board of governors. The appointed members shall be confirmed by the senate and serve staggered terms of five years as provided by law. The chair of the faculty senate, or the equivalent, and the president of the student body of the university shall also be members.

(d) Statewide Board of Governors.
The board of governors shall be a body corporate consisting of seventeen members. The board shall operate, regulate, control, and be fully responsible for the management of the whole university system. These responsibilities shall include, but not be limited to, defining the distinctive mission of each constituent university and its articulation with free public schools and community colleges, ensuring the well-planned coordination and operation of the system, and avoiding wasteful duplication of facilities or programs. The board's management shall be subject to the powers of the legislature to appropriate for the expenditure of funds, and the board shall account for such expenditures as provided by law. The governor shall appoint to the board fourteen citizens dedicated to the purposes of the state university system. The appointed members shall be confirmed by the senate and serve staggered terms of seven years as provided by law. The commissioner of education, the chair of the advisory council of faculty senates, or the equivalent, and the president of the Florida student association, or the

equivalent, shall also be members of the board.

ARTICLE X: MISCELLANEOUS

Section 1. Amendments to United States Constitution

The legislature shall not take action on any proposed amendment to the constitution of the United States unless a majority of the members thereof have been elected after the proposed amendment has been submitted for ratification.

Section 2. Militia

(a) The militia shall be composed of all ablebodied inhabitants of the state who are or have declared their intention to become citizens of the United States; and no person because of religious creed or opinion shall be exempted from military duty except upon conditions provided by law.
(b) The organizing, equipping, housing, maintaining, and disciplining of the militia, and the safekeeping of public arms may be provided for by law.
(c) The governor shall appoint all commissioned officers of the militia, including an adjutant general who shall be chief of staff. The appointment of all general officers shall be subject to confirmation by the senate.
(d) The qualifications of personnel and officers of the federally recognized national guard, including the adjutant general, and the grounds and proceedings for their discipline and removal shall conform to the appropriate United States army or air force regulations and usages.

Section 3. Vacancy in Office

Vacancy in office shall occur upon the creation of an office, upon the death, removal from office, or resignation of the incumbent or the incumbent's succession to another office, unexplained absence for sixty consecutive days, or failure to maintain the residence required when elected or appointed, and upon failure of one elected or appointed to office to qualify within thirty days from the commencement of the term.

Section 4. Homestead; Exemptions

(a) There shall be exempt from forced sale under process of any court, and no judgment, decree or execution shall be a lien thereon, except for the payment of taxes and assessments thereon, obligations contracted for the purchase, improvement or repair thereof, or obligations contracted for house, field or other labor performed on the realty, the following property owned by a natural person:

(1) a homestead, if located outside a municipality, to the extent of one hundred sixty acres of contiguous land and improvements thereon, which shall not be reduced without the owner's consent by reason of subsequent inclusion in a municipality; or if located within a municipality, to the extent of one-half acre of contiguous land, upon which the exemption shall be limited to the residence of the owner or the owner's family;
(2) personal property to the value of one thousand dollars.

(b) These exemptions shall inure to the surviving spouse or heirs of the owner.
(c) The homestead shall not be subject to devise if the owner is survived by spouse or minor child, except the homestead may be devised to the owner's spouse if there be no minor child. The owner of homestead real estate, joined by the spouse if married, may alienate the homestead by mortgage, sale or gift and, if married, may by deed transfer the title to an estate by the entirety with the spouse. If the owner or spouse is incompetent, the method of alienation or encumbrance shall be as provided by law.

Section 5. Coverture and Property
There shall be no distinction between married women and married men in the holding, control, disposition, or encumbering of their property, both real and personal; except that dower or curtesy may be established and regulated by law.

Section 6. Eminent Domain

(a) No private property shall be taken except for a public purpose and with full compensation therefor paid to each owner or secured by deposit in the registry of the court and available to the owner.
(b) Provision may be made by law for the taking of easements, by like proceedings, for the drainage of the land of one person over or through the land of another.
(c) Private property taken by eminent domain pursuant to a petition to initiate condemnation proceedings filed on or after January 2, 2007, may not be conveyed to a natural person or private entity except as provided by general law passed by a three-fifths vote of the membership of each house of the Legislature.

Section 7. Lotteries

Lotteries, other than the types of pari-mutuel pools authorized by law as of the effective date of this constitution, are hereby prohibited in this state.

Section 8. Census

(a) Each decennial census of the state taken by the United States shall be an official census of the state.
(b) Each decennial census, for the purpose of classifications based upon population, shall become effective on the thirtieth day after the final adjournment of the regular session of the legislature convened next after certification of the census.

Section 9. Repeal of Criminal Statutes

Repeal or amendment of a criminal statute shall not affect prosecution or punishment for any crime previously committed.

Section 10. Felony; Definition

The term "felony" as used herein and in the laws of this state shall mean any criminal offense that is punishable under the laws of this state, or that would be punishable if committed in this state, by death or by imprisonment in the state penitentiary.

Section 11. Sovereignty Lands
The title to lands under navigable waters, within the boundaries of the state, which have not been alienated, including beaches below mean high water lines, is held by the state, by virtue of its sovereignty, in trust for all the people. Sale of such lands may be authorized by law, but only when in the public interest. Private use of portions of such lands may be authorized by law, but only when not contrary to the public interest.

Section 12. Rules of Construction
Unless qualified in the text the following rules of construction shall apply to this constitution.

(a) "Herein" refers to the entire constitution.
(b) The singular includes the plural.
(c) The masculine includes the feminine.
(d) "Vote of the electors" means the vote of the majority of those voting on the matter in an election, general or special, in which those participating are limited to the electors of the governmental unit referred to in the text.
(e) Vote or other action of a legislative house or other governmental body means the vote or action of a majority or other specified percentage of those members voting on the matter. "Of the membership" means "of all members thereof."
(f) The terms "judicial office," "justices" and "judges" shall not include judges of courts established solely for the trial of violations of ordinances.
(g) "Special law" means a special or local law.
(h) Titles and subtitles shall not be used in construction.

Section 13. Suits Against the State
Provision may be made by general law for bringing suit against the state as to all liabilities now existing or hereafter originating.

Section 14. State Retirement Systems Benefit Changes

A governmental unit responsible for any retirement or pension system supported in whole or in part by public funds shall not after January 1, 1977, provide any increase in the benefits to the members or beneficiaries of such system unless such unit has made or concurrently makes provision for the funding of the increase in benefits on a sound actuarial basis.

Section 15. State operated lotteries

(a) Lotteries may be operated by the state.
(b) If any subsection or subsections of the amendment to the Florida Constitution are held unconstitutional for containing more than one subject, this amendment shall be limited to subsection (a) above.
(c) This amendment shall be implemented as follows:

(1) Schedule—On the effective date of this amendment, the lotteries shall be known as the Florida Education Lotteries. Net proceeds derived from the lotteries shall be deposited to a state trust fund, to be designated The State Education Lotteries Trust Fund, to be appropriated by the Legislature. The schedule may be amended by general law.

Section 16. Limiting Marine Net Fishing

(a) The marine resources of the State of Florida belong to all of the people of the state and should be conserved and managed for the benefit of the state, its people, and future generations. To this end the people hereby enact limitations on marine net fishing in Florida waters to protect saltwater finfish, shellfish, and other marine animals from unnecessary killing, overfishing and waste.
(b) For the purpose of catching or taking any saltwater finfish, shellfish or other marine animals in Florida waters:

(1) No gill nets or other entangling nets shall be used in any Florida waters; and

(2) In addition to the prohibition set forth in (1), no other type of net containing more than 500 square feet of mesh area shall be used in nearshore and inshore Florida waters. Additionally, no more than two such nets, which shall not be connected, shall be used from any vessel, and no person not on a vessel shall use more than one such net in nearshore and inshore Florida waters.

(c) For purposes of this section:

(1) "gill net" means one or more walls of netting which captures saltwater finfish by ensnaring or entangling them in the meshes of the net by the gills, and "entangling net" means a drift net, trammell net, stab net, or any other net which captures saltwater finfish, shellfish, or other marine animals by causing all or part of heads, fins, legs, or other body parts to become entangled or ensnared in the meshes of the net, but a hand thrown cast net is not a gill net or an entangling net;

(2) "mesh area" of a net means the total area of netting with the meshes open to comprise the maximum square footage. The square footage shall be calculated using standard mathematical formulas for geometric shapes. Seines and other rectangular nets shall be calculated using the maximum length and maximum width of the netting. Trawls and other bag type nets shall be calculated as a cone using the maximum circumference of the net mouth to derive the radius, and the maximum length from the net mouth to the tail end of the net to derive the slant height. Calculations for any other nets or combination type nets shall be based on the shapes of the individual components;

(3) "coastline" means the territorial sea base line for the State of Florida established pursuant to the laws of the United States of America;

(4) "Florida waters" means the waters of the Atlantic Ocean, the Gulf of Mexico, the Straits of Florida, and any other bodies of water under the jurisdiction of the State of Florida, whether coastal, intracoastal or inland, and any part thereof; and

(5) "nearshore and inshore Florida waters" means all Florida waters inside a line three miles seaward of the coastline along the Gulf of Mexico and inside a line one mile seaward of the coastline along the Atlantic Ocean.

(d) This section shall not apply to the use of nets for scientific research or governmental purposes.

(e) Persons violating this section shall be prosecuted and punished pursuant to the penalties provided in section 370.021(2)(a),(b),(c)6. and 7., and (e), Florida Statutes (1991), unless and until the legislature enacts more stringent penalties for violations hereof. On and after the effective date of this section, law enforcement officers in the state are authorized to enforce the provisions of this section in the same manner and authority as if a violation of this section constituted a violation of Chapter 370, Florida Statutes (1991).

(f) It is the intent of this section that implementing legislation is not required for enforcing any violations hereof, but nothing in this section prohibits the establishment by law or pursuant to law of more restrictions on the use of nets for the purpose of catching or taking any saltwater finfish, shellfish, or other marine animals.

(g) If any portion of this section is held invalid for any reason, the remaining portion of this section, to the fullest extent possible, shall be severed from the void portion and given the fullest possible force and application.

(h) This section shall take effect on the July 1 next occurring after approval hereof by vote of the electors.

Section 17. Everglades Trust Fund

(a) There is hereby established the Everglades Trust Fund, which shall not be subject to termination pursuant to Article III, Section 19(f). The purpose of the Everglades Trust Fund is to make funds available to assist in conservation and protection of natural resources and abatement of water pollution in the Everglades Protection Area and the Everglades Agricultural Area. The trust fund shall be administered by the South Florida Water Management District, or its successor agency, consistent with statutory law.

(b) The Everglades Trust Fund may receive funds from any source, including gifts from individuals, corporations or other entities; funds from general revenue as determined by the Legislature; and any other funds so designated by the Legislature, by the United States Congress or by any other governmental entity.
(c) Funds deposited to the Everglades Trust Fund shall be expended for purposes of conservation and protection of natural resources and abatement of water pollution in the Everglades Protection Area and Everglades Agricultural Area.
(d) For purposes of this subsection, the terms "Everglades Protection Area," "Everglades Agricultural Area" and "South Florida Water Management District" shall have the meanings as defined in statutes in effect on January 1, 1996.

Section 18. Disposition of conservation lands
The fee interest in real property held by an entity of the state and designated for natural resources conservation purposes as provided by general law shall be managed for the benefit of the citizens of this state and may be disposed of only if the members of the governing board of the entity holding title determine the property is no longer needed for conservation purposes and only upon a vote of two-thirds of the governing board.

Section 19. High speed ground transportation system
To reduce traffic congestion and provide alternatives to the traveling public, it is hereby declared to be in the public interest that a high speed ground transportation system consisting of a monorail, fixed guideway or magnetic levitation system, capable of speeds in excess of 120 miles per hour, be developed and operated in the State of Florida to provide high speed ground transportation by innovative, efficient and effective technologies consisting of dedicated rails or guideways separated from motor vehicular traffic that will link the five largest urban areas of the State as determined by the Legislature and provide for access to existing air and ground transportation facilities and services. The Legislature, the Cabinet and the Governor are hereby directed to proceed with the development of such a system by the State

and/or by a private entity pursuant to state approval and authorization, including the acquisition of right-of-way, the financing of design and construction of the system, and the operation of the system, as provided by specific appropriation and by law, with construction to begin on or before November 1, 2003.

Section 20. Workplaces Without Tobacco Smoke

(a) Prohibition.
As a Florida health initiative to protect people from the health hazards of second-hand tobacco smoke, tobacco smoking is prohibited in enclosed indoor workplaces.

(b) Exceptions.
As further explained in the definitions below, tobacco smoking may be permitted in private residences whenever they are not being used commercially to provide child care, adult care, or health care, or any combination thereof; and further may be permitted in retail tobacco shops, designated smoking guest rooms at hotels and other public lodging establishments; and stand-alone bars. However, nothing in this section or in its implementing legislation or regulations shall prohibit the owner, lessee, or other person in control of the use of an enclosed indoor workplace from further prohibiting or limiting smoking therein.

(c) Definitions.
For purposes of this section, the following words and terms shall have the stated meanings:

(1) "Smoking" means inhaling, exhaling, burning, carrying, or possessing any lighted tobacco product, including cigarettes, cigars, pipe tobacco, and any other lighted tobacco product.
(2) "Second-hand smoke," also known as environmental tobacco smoke (ETS), means smoke emitted from lighted, smoldering, or burning tobacco when the smoker is not inhaling; smoke emitted at the mouthpiece during puff drawing; and smoke exhaled by

the smoker.

(3) "Work" means any person's providing any employment or employment-type service for or at the request of another individual or individuals or any public or private entity, whether for compensation or not, whether full or part-time, whether legally or not. "Work" includes, without limitation, any such service performed by an employee, independent contractor, agent, partner, proprietor, manager, officer, director, apprentice, trainee, associate, servant, volunteer, and the like.

(4) "Enclosed indoor workplace" means any place where one or more persons engages in work, and which place is predominantly or totally bounded on all sides and above by physical barriers, regardless of whether such barriers consist of or include uncovered openings, screened or otherwise partially covered openings; or open or closed windows, jalousies, doors, or the like. This section applies to all such enclosed indoor workplaces without regard to whether work is occurring at any given time.

(5) "Commercial" use of a private residence means any time during which the owner, lessee, or other person occupying or controlling the use of the private residence is furnishing in the private residence, or causing or allowing to be furnished in the private residence, child care, adult care, or health care, or any combination thereof, and receiving or expecting to receive compensation therefor.

(6) "Retail tobacco shop" means any enclosed indoor workplace dedicated to or predominantly for the retail sale of tobacco, tobacco products, and accessories for such products, in which the sale of other products or services is merely incidental.

(7) "Designated smoking guest rooms at public lodging establishments" means the sleeping rooms and directly associated private areas, such as bathrooms, living rooms, and kitchen areas, if any, rented to guests for their exclusive transient occupancy in public lodging establishments including hotels, motels, resort condominiums, transient apartments, transient lodging establishments, rooming houses, boarding houses, resort dwellings, bed and breakfast inns, and the like; and designated by the person or persons having management authority over such public lodging establishment as rooms in which smoking may be permitted.

(8) "Stand-alone bar" means any place of business devoted during any time of operation predominantly or totally to serving alcoholic beverages, intoxicating beverages, or intoxicating liquors, or any combination thereof, for consumption on the licensed premises; in which the serving of food, if any, is merely incidental to the consumption of any such beverage; and that is not located within, and does not share any common entryway or common indoor area with, any other enclosed indoor workplace including any business for which the sale of food or any other product or service is more than an incidental source of gross revenue.

(d) Legislation.

In the next regular legislative session occurring after voter approval of this amendment, the Florida Legislature shall adopt legislation to implement this amendment in a manner consistent with its broad purpose and stated terms, and having an effective date no later than July 1 of the year following voter approval. Such legislation shall include, without limitation, civil penalties for violations of this section; provisions for administrative enforcement; and the requirement and authorization of agency rules for implementation and enforcement. Nothing herein shall preclude the Legislature from enacting any law constituting or allowing a more restrictive regulation of tobacco smoking than is provided in this section.

Section 21. Limiting Cruel And Inhumane Confinement Of Pigs During Pregnancy

Inhumane treatment of animals is a concern of Florida citizens. To prevent cruelty to certain animals and as recommended by The Humane Society of the United States, the people of the State of Florida hereby limit the cruel and inhumane confinement of pigs during pregnancy as provided herein.

(a) It shall be unlawful for any person to confine a pig during pregnancy in an enclosure, or to tether a pig during pregnancy, on a farm in such a way that she is prevented from turning around freely.
(b) This section shall not apply:

(1) when a pig is undergoing an examination, test, treatment or operation carried out for veterinary purposes, provided the period during which the animal is confined or tethered is not longer than reasonably necessary.
(2) during the prebirthing period.

(c) For purposes of this section:

(1) "enclosure" means any cage, crate or other enclosure in which a pig is kept for all or the majority of any day, including what is commonly described as the "gestation crate."
(2) "farm" means the land, buildings, support facilities, and other appurtenances used in the production of animals for food or fiber.
(3) "person" means any natural person, corporation and/or business entity.
(4) "pig" means any animal of the porcine species.
(5) "turning around freely" means turning around without having to touch any side of the pig's enclosure.
(6) "prebirthing period" means the seven day period prior to a pig's expected date of giving birth.

(d) A person who violates this section shall be guilty of a misdemeanor of the first degree, punishable as provided in s. 775.082(4)(a), Florida Statutes (1999), as amended, or by a fine of not more than $5000, or by both imprisonment and a fine, unless and until the legislature enacts more stringent penalties for violations hereof. On and after the effective date of this section, law enforcement officers in the state are authorized to enforce the provisions of this section in the same manner and authority as if a violation of this section constituted a violation of Section 828.13, Florida Statutes (1999). The confinement or

tethering of each pig shall constitute a separate offense. The knowledge or acts of agents and employees of a person in regard to a pig owned, farmed or in the custody of a person, shall be held to be the knowledge or act of such person.
(e) It is the intent of this section that implementing legislation is not required for enforcing any violations hereof.
(f) If any portion of this section is held invalid for any reason, the remaining portion of this section, to the fullest extent possible, shall be severed from the void portion and given the fullest possible force and application.
(g) This section shall take effect six years after approval by the electors.

Section 22. Parental Notice of Termination of a Minor's Pregnancy

The Legislature shall not limit or deny the privacy right guaranteed to a minor under the United States Constitution as interpreted by the United States Supreme Court. Notwithstanding a minor's right of privacy provided in Section 23 of Article I, the Legislature is authorized to require by general law for notification to a parent or guardian of a minor before the termination of the minor's pregnancy. The Legislature shall provide exceptions to such requirement for notification and shall create a process for judicial waiver of the notification.

Section 23. Slot Machines

(a) After voter approval of this constitutional amendment, the governing bodies of Miami-Dade and Broward Counties each may hold a county-wide referendum in their respective counties on whether to authorize slot machines within existing, licensed parimutuel facilities (thoroughbred and harness racing, greyhound racing, and jai-alai) that have conducted live racing or games in that county during each of the last two calendar years before the effective date of this amendment. If the voters of such county approve the referendum question by majority vote, slot machines shall be authorized in such parimutuel facilities. If the voters of such county by majority vote disapprove the referendum question, slot machines shall not be so authorized, and the question shall not be presented in another referendum in that county for at least two years.

(b) In the next regular Legislative session occurring after voter approval of this constitutional amendment, the Legislature shall adopt legislation implementing this section and having an effective date no later than July 1 of the year following voter approval of this amendment. Such legislation shall authorize agency rules for implementation, and may include provisions for the licensure and regulation of slot machines. The Legislature may tax slot machine revenues, and any such taxes must supplement public education funding statewide.

(c) If any part of this section is held invalid for any reason, the remaining portion or portions shall be severed from the invalid portion and given the fullest possible force and effect.

(d) This amendment shall become effective when approved by vote of the electors of the state.

Section 24. Florida Minimum Wage

(a) Public Policy.
All working Floridians are entitled to be paid a minimum wage that is sufficient to provide a decent and healthy life for them and their families, that protects their employers from unfair low-wage competition, and that does not force them to rely on taxpayer-funded public services in order to avoid economic hardship.

(b) Definitions
As used in this amendment, the terms "Employer," "Employee" and "Wage" shall have the meanings established under the federal Fair Labor Standards Act (FLSA) and its implementing regulations.

(c) Minimum Wage
Employers shall pay Employees Wages no less than the Minimum Wage for all hours worked in Florida. Six months after enactment, the Minimum Wage shall be established at an hourly

rate of $6.15. On September 30th of that year and on each following September 30th, the state Agency for Workforce Innovation shall calculate an adjusted Minimum Wage rate by increasing the current Minimum Wage rate by the rate of inflation during the twelve months prior to each September 1st using the consumer price index for urban wage earners and clerical workers, CPI-W, or a successor index as calculated by the United States Department of Labor. Each adjusted Minimum Wage rate calculated shall be published and take effect on the following January 1st. For tipped Employees meeting eligibility requirements for the tip credit under the FLSA, Employers may credit towards satisfaction of the Minimum Wage tips up to the amount of the allowable FLSA tip credit in 2003.

(d) Retaliation Prohibited.
It shall be unlawful for an Employer or any other party to discriminate in any manner or take adverse action against any person in retaliation for exercising rights protected under this amendment. Rights protected under this amendment include, but are not limited to, the right to file a complaint or inform any person about any party's alleged noncompliance with this amendment, and the right to inform any person of his or her potential rights under this amendment and to assist him or her in asserting such rights.

(e) Enforcement.
Persons aggrieved by a violation of this amendment may bring a civil action in a court of competent jurisdiction against an Employer or person violating this amendment and, upon prevailing, shall recover the full amount of any back wages unlawfully withheld plus the same amount as liquidated damages, and shall be awarded reasonable attorney's fees and costs. In addition, they shall be entitled to such legal or equitable relief as may be appropriate to remedy the violation including, without limitation, reinstatement in employment and/or injunctive relief. Any Employer or other person found liable for willfully violating this amendment shall also be subject to a fine payable to the state in the amount of $1000.00 for each

violation. The state attorney general or other official designated by the state legislature may also bring a civil action to enforce this amendment. Actions to enforce this amendment shall be subject to a statute of limitations of four years or, in the case of willful violations, five years. Such actions may be brought as a class action pursuant to Rule 1.220 of the Florida Rules of Civil Procedure.

(f) Additional Legislation, Implementation and Construction.
Implementing legislation is not required in order to enforce this amendment. The state legislature may by statute establish additional remedies or fines for violations of this amendment, raise the applicable Minimum Wage rate, reduce the tip credit, or extend coverage of the Minimum Wage to employers or employees not covered by this amendment. The state legislature may by statute or the state Agency for Workforce Innovation may by regulation adopt any measures appropriate for the implementation of this amendment. This amendment provides for payment of a minimum wage and shall not be construed to preempt or otherwise limit the authority of the state legislature or any other public body to adopt or enforce any other law, regulation, requirement, policy or standard that provides for payment of higher or supplemental wages or benefits, or that extends such protections to employers or employees not covered by this amendment. It is intended that case law, administrative interpretations, and other guiding standards developed under the federal FLSA shall guide the construction of this amendment and any implementing statutes or regulations.

(g) Severability.
If any part of this amendment, or the application of this amendment to any person or circumstance, is held invalid, the remainder of this amendment, including the application of such part to other persons or circumstances, shall not be affected by such a holding and shall continue in full force and effect. To this end, the parts of this amendment are severable.

Section 25. Patients' Right To Know About Adverse Medical Incidents

(a) In addition to any other similar rights provided herein or by general law, patients have a right to have access to any records made or received in the course of business by a health care facility or provider relating to any adverse medical incident.
(b) In providing such access, the identity of patients involved in the incidents shall not be disclosed, and any privacy restrictions imposed by federal law shall be maintained.
(c) For purposes of this section, the following terms have the following meanings:

(1) The phrases "health care facility" and "health care provider" have the meaning given in general law related to a patient's rights and responsibilities.
(2) The term "patient" means an individual who has sought, is seeking, is undergoing, or has undergone care or treatment in a health care facility or by a health care provider.
(3) The phrase "adverse medical incident" means medical negligence, intentional misconduct, and any other act, neglect, or default of a health care facility or health care provider that caused or could have caused injury to or death of a patient, including, but not limited to, those incidents that are required by state or federal law to be reported to any governmental agency or body, and incidents that are reported to or reviewed by any health care facility peer review, risk management, quality assurance, credentials, or similar committee, or any representative of any such committees.
(4) The phrase "have access to any records" means, in addition to any other procedure for producing such records provided by general law, making the records available for inspection and copying upon formal or informal request by the patient or a representative of the patient, provided that current records which have been made publicly available by publication or on the Internet may be "provided" by reference to the location at which the records are publicly available.

Section 26. Prohibition of Medical License After Repeated Medical Malpractice

(a) No person who has been found to have committed three or more incidents of medical malpractice shall be licensed or continue to be licensed by the State of Florida to provide health care services as a medical doctor.
(b) For purposes of this section, the following terms have the following meanings:

(1) The phrase "medical malpractice" means both the failure to practice medicine in Florida with that level of care, skill, and treatment recognized in general law related to health care providers' licensure, and any similar wrongful act, neglect, or default in other states or countries which, if committed in Florida, would have been considered medical malpractice.
(2) The phrase "found to have committed" means that the malpractice has been found in a final judgment of a court of law, final administrative agency decision, or decision of binding arbitration.

Section 27. Comprehensive Statewide Tobacco Education and Prevention Program

In order to protect people, especially youth, from health hazards of using tobacco, including addictive disorders, cancer, cardiovascular diseases, and lung diseases; and to discourage use of tobacco, particularly among youth, a portion of the money that tobacco companies pay to the State of Florida under the Tobacco Settlement each year shall be used to fund a comprehensive statewide tobacco education and prevention program consistent with recommendations of the U.S. Centers for Disease Control and Prevention (CDC), as follows:

(a) Program.

The money appropriated pursuant to this section shall be used to fund a comprehensive statewide tobacco education and prevention program consistent with the recommendations for effective program components in the 1999 Best Practices for

Comprehensive Tobacco Control Programs of the CDC, as such Best Practices may be amended by the CDC. This program shall include, at a minimum, the following components, and may include additional components that are also contained within the CDC Best Practices, as periodically amended, and that are effective at accomplishing the purpose of this section, and that do not undermine the effectiveness of these required minimum components:

(1) an advertising campaign to discourage the use of tobacco and to educate people, especially youth, about the health hazards of tobacco, which shall be designed to be effective at achieving these goals and shall include, but need not be limited to, television, radio, and print advertising, with no limitations on any individual advertising medium utilized; and which shall be funded at a level equivalent to one-third of each total annual appropriation required by this section;

(2) evidence-based curricula and programs to educate youth about tobacco and to discourage their use of it, including, but not limited to, programs that involve youth, educate youth about the health hazards of tobacco, help youth develop skills to refuse tobacco, and demonstrate to youth how to stop using tobacco;

(3) programs of local community-based partnerships that discourage the use of tobacco and work to educate people, especially youth, about the health hazards of tobacco, with an emphasis on programs that involve youth and emphasize the prevention and cessation of tobacco use;

(4) enforcement of laws, regulations, and policies against the sale or other provision of tobacco to minors, and the possession of tobacco by minors; and

(5) publicly-reported annual evaluations to ensure that moneys appropriated pursuant to this section are spent properly, which shall include evaluation of the program's effectiveness in reducing and preventing tobacco use, and annual recommendations for improvements to enhance the program's effectiveness, which are to include comparisons to similar programs proven to be effective in other states, as well as comparisons to CDC Best Practices, including amendments thereto.

(b) Funding.
In every year beginning with the calendar year after voters approve this amendment, the Florida Legislature shall appropriate, for the purpose expressed herein, from the total gross funds that tobacco companies pay to the State of Florida under the Tobacco Settlement, an amount equal to fifteen percent of such funds paid to the State in 2005; and the appropriation required by this section shall be adjusted annually for inflation, using the Consumer Price Index as published by the United States Department of Labor.

(c) Definitions.
"Tobacco" includes, without limitation, tobacco itself and tobacco products that include tobacco and are intended or expected for human use or consumption, including, but not limited to, cigarettes, cigars, pipe tobacco, and smokeless tobacco. The "Tobacco Settlement" means that certain Settlement Agreement dated August 25, 1997, entered into in settlement of the case styled as State of Florida, et al. v. American Tobacco Company, et al., Case No. 95-1466 AH (Fla. 15th Cir. Ct.), as amended by Stipulation of Amendment dated September 11, 1998; and includes any subsequent amendments and successor agreements. "Youth" includes minors and young adults.

(d) Effective Date.
This amendment shall become effective immediately upon approval by the voters.

Section 28. Land Acquisition Trust Fund

(a) Effective on July 1 of the year following passage of this amendment by the voters, and for a period of 20 years after that effective date, the Land Acquisition Trust Fund shall receive no less than 33 percent of net revenues derived from the existing excise tax on documents, as defined in the statutes in effect on January 1, 2012, as amended from time to time, or any successor or replacement tax, after the Department of Revenue first deducts a service charge to pay the costs of the collection

and enforcement of the excise tax on documents.
(b) Funds in the Land Acquisition Trust Fund shall be expended only for the following purposes:

(1) As provided by law, to finance or refinance: the acquisition and improvement of land, water areas, and related property interests, including conservation easements, and resources for conservation lands including wetlands, forests, and fish and wildlife habitat; wildlife management areas; lands that protect water resources and drinking water sources, including lands protecting the water quality and quantity of rivers, lakes, streams, springsheds, and lands providing recharge for groundwater and aquifer systems; lands in the Everglades Agricultural Area and the Everglades Protection Area, as defined in Article II, Section 7(b); beaches and shores; outdoor recreation lands, including recreational trails, parks, and urban open space; rural landscapes; working farms and ranches; historic or geologic sites; together with management, restoration of natural systems, and the enhancement of public access or recreational enjoyment of conservation lands.
(2) To pay the debt service on bonds issued pursuant to Article VII, Section 11(e).

(c) The moneys deposited into the Land Acquisition Trust Fund, as defined by the statutes in effect on January 1, 2012, shall not be or become commingled with the general revenue fund of the state.

Section 29. Medical Marijuana Production, Possession and Use

(a) Public Policy.

(1) The medical use of marijuana by a qualifying patient or caregiver in compliance with this section is not subject to criminal or civil liability or sanctions under Florida law.

(2) A physician shall not be subject to criminal or civil liability or sanctions under Florida law solely for issuing a physician certification with reasonable care to a person diagnosed with a debilitating medical condition in compliance with this section.
(3) Actions and conduct by a Medical Marijuana Treatment Center registered with the Department, or its agents or employees, and in compliance with this section and Department regulations, shall not be subject to criminal or civil liability or sanctions under Florida law.

(b) Definitions.
For purposes of this section, the following words and terms shall have the following meanings:

(1) "Debilitating Medical Condition" means cancer, epilepsy, glaucoma, positive status for human immunodeficiency virus (HIV), acquired immune deficiency syndrome (AIDS), post-traumatic stress disorder (PTSD), amyotrophic lateral sclerosis (ALS), Crohn's disease, Parkinson's disease, multiple sclerosis, or other debilitating medical conditions of the same kind or class as or comparable to those enumerated, and for which a physician believes that the medical use of marijuana would likely outweigh the potential health risks for a patient.
(2) "Department" means the Department of Health or its successor agency.
(3) "Identification card" means a document issued by the Department that identifies a qualifying patient or a caregiver.
(4) "Marijuana" has the meaning given cannabis in Section 893.02(3), Florida Statutes (2014), and, in addition, "Low-THC cannabis" as defined in Section 381.986(1)(b), Florida Statutes (2014), shall also be included in the meaning of the term "marijuana."
(5) "Medical Marijuana Treatment Center" (MMTC) means an entity that acquires, cultivates, possesses, processes (including development of related products such as food, tinctures, aerosols, oils, or ointments), transfers, transports, sells, distributes, dispenses, or administers marijuana, products containing marijuana, related supplies, or educational materials

to qualifying patients or their caregivers and is registered by the Department.

(6) "Medical use" means the acquisition, possession, use, delivery, transfer, or administration of an amount of marijuana not in conflict with Department rules, or of related supplies by a qualifying patient or caregiver for use by the caregiver's designated qualifying patient for the treatment of a debilitating medical condition.

(7) "Caregiver" means a person who is at least twenty-one (21) years old who has agreed to assist with a qualifying patient's medical use of marijuana and has qualified for and obtained a caregiver identification card issued by the Department. The Department may limit the number of qualifying patients a caregiver may assist at one time and the number of caregivers that a qualifying patient may have at one time. Caregivers are prohibited from consuming marijuana obtained for medical use by the qualifying patient.

(8) "Physician" means a person who is licensed to practice medicine in Florida.

(9) "Physician certification" means a written document signed by a physician, stating that in the physician's professional opinion, the patient suffers from a debilitating medical condition, that the medical use of marijuana would likely outweigh the potential health risks for the patient, and for how long the physician recommends the medical use of marijuana for the patient. A physician certification may only be provided after the physician has conducted a physical examination and a full assessment of the medical history of the patient. In order for a physician certification to be issued to a minor, a parent or legal guardian of the minor must consent in writing.

(10) "Qualifying patient" means a person who has been diagnosed to have a debilitating medical condition, who has a physician certification and a valid qualifying patient identification card. If the Department does not begin issuing identification cards within nine (9) months after the effective date of this section, then a valid physician certification will serve as a patient identification card in order to allow a person to become a "qualifying patient" until the Department begins issuing identification cards.

(c) Limitations.

(1) Nothing in this section allows for a violation of any law other than for conduct in compliance with the provisions of this section.
(2) Nothing in this section shall affect or repeal laws relating to non-medical use, possession, production, or sale of marijuana.
(3) Nothing in this section authorizes the use of medical marijuana by anyone other than a qualifying patient.
(4) Nothing in this section shall permit the operation of any vehicle, aircraft, train or boat while under the influence of marijuana.
(5) Nothing in this section requires the violation of federal law or purports to give immunity under federal law.
(6) Nothing in this section shall require any accommodation of any on-site medical use of marijuana in any correctional institution or detention facility or place of education or employment, or of smoking medical marijuana in any public place.
(7) Nothing in this section shall require any health insurance provider or any government agency or authority to reimburse any person for expenses related to the medical use of marijuana.
(8) Nothing in this section shall affect or repeal laws relating to negligence or professional malpractice on the part of a qualified patient, caregiver, physician, MMTC, or its agents or employees.

(d) Duties of the Department.
The Department shall issue reasonable regulations necessary for the implementation and enforcement of this section. The purpose of the regulations is to ensure the availability and safe use of medical marijuana by qualifying patients. It is the duty of the Department to promulgate regulations in a timely fashion.

(1) Implementing Regulations. In order to allow the Department sufficient time after passage of this section, the following regulations shall be promulgated no later than six (6) months after the effective date of this section:

a. Procedures for the issuance and annual renewal of qualifying patient identification cards to people with physician certifications and standards for renewal of such identification cards. Before issuing an identification card to a minor, the Department must receive written consent from the minor's parent or legal guardian, in addition to the physician certification.
b. Procedures establishing qualifications and standards for caregivers, including conducting appropriate background checks, and procedures for the issuance and annual renewal of caregiver identification cards.
c. Procedures for the registration of MMTCs that include procedures for the issuance, renewal, suspension and revocation of registration, and standards to ensure proper security, record keeping, testing, labeling, inspection, and safety.
d. A regulation that defines the amount of marijuana that could reasonably be presumed to be an adequate supply for qualifying patients' medical use, based on the best available evidence. This presumption as to quantity may be overcome with evidence of a particular qualifying patient's appropriate medical use.

(2) Identification cards and registrations. The Department shall begin issuing qualifying patient and caregiver identification cards, and registering MMTCs no later than nine (9) months after the effective date of this section.
(3) If the Department does not issue regulations, or if the Department does not begin issuing identification cards and registering MMTCs within the time limits set in this section, any Florida citizen shall have standing to seek judicial relief to compel compliance with the Department's constitutional duties.
(4) The Department shall protect the confidentiality of all qualifying patients. All records containing the identity of qualifying patients shall be confidential and kept from public disclosure other than for valid medical or law enforcement

purposes.

(e) Legislation.
Nothing in this section shall limit the legislature from enacting laws consistent with this section.

(f) Severability.
The provisions of this section are severable and if any clause, sentence, paragraph or section of this measure, or an application thereof, is adjudged invalid by a court of competent jurisdiction other provisions shall continue to be in effect to the fullest extent possible.

ARTICLE XI: AMENDMENTS

Section 1. Proposal by Legislature

Amendment of a section or revision of one or more articles, or the whole, of this constitution may be proposed by joint resolution agreed to by three-fifths of the membership of each house of the legislature. The full text of the joint resolution and the vote of each member voting shall be entered on the journal of each house.

Section 2. Revision commission

(a) Within thirty days before the convening of the 2017 regular session of the legislature, and each twentieth year thereafter, there shall be established a constitution revision commission composed of the following thirty-seven members:

(1) the attorney general of the state;
(2) fifteen members selected by the governor;
(3) nine members selected by the speaker of the house of representatives and nine members selected by the president of the senate; and
(4) three members selected by the chief justice of the supreme court of Florida with the advice of the justices.

(b) The governor shall designate one member of the commission as its chair. Vacancies in the membership of the commission shall be filled in the same manner as the original appointments.

(c) Each constitution revision commission shall convene at the call of its chair, adopt its rules of procedure, examine the constitution of the state, hold public hearings, and, not later than one hundred eighty days prior to the next general election, file with the custodian of state records its proposal, if any, of a revision of this constitution or any part of it.

Section 3. Initiative
The power to propose the revision or amendment of any portion or portions of this constitution by initiative is reserved to the people, provided that, any such revision or amendment, except for those limiting the power of government to raise revenue, shall embrace but one subject and matter directly connected therewith. It may be invoked by filing with the custodian of state records a petition containing a copy of the proposed revision or amendment, signed by a number of electors in each of one half of the congressional districts of the state, and of the state as a whole, equal to eight percent of the votes cast in each of such districts respectively and in the state as a whole in the last preceding election in which presidential electors were chosen.

Section 4. Constitutional Convention

(a) The power to call a convention to consider a revision of the entire constitution is reserved to the people. It may be invoked by filing with the custodian of state records a petition, containing a declaration that a constitutional convention is desired, signed by a number of electors in each of one half of the congressional districts of the state, and of the state as a whole, equal to fifteen per cent of the votes cast in each such district respectively and in the state as a whole in the last preceding election of presidential electors.
(b) At the next general election held more than ninety days after the filing of such petition there shall be submitted to the electors of the state the question: "Shall a constitutional convention be held?" If a majority voting on the question votes in the affirmative, at the next succeeding general election there shall be elected from each representative district a member of a constitutional convention. On the twenty-first day following that election, the convention shall sit at the capital, elect officers, adopt rules of procedure, judge the election of its membership, and fix a time and place for its future meetings. Not later than ninety days before the next succeeding general election, the convention shall cause to be filed with the custodian of state records any revision of this constitution proposed by it.

Section 5. Amendment or Revision Election

(a) A proposed amendment to or revision of this constitution, or any part of it, shall be submitted to the electors at the next general election held more than ninety days after the joint resolution or report of revision commission, constitutional convention or taxation and budget reform commission proposing it is filed with the custodian of state records, unless, pursuant to law enacted by the affirmative vote of three-fourths of the membership of each house of the legislature and limited to a single amendment or revision, it is submitted at an earlier special election held more than ninety days after such filing.
(b) A proposed amendment or revision of this constitution, or any part of it, by initiative shall be submitted to the electors at the general election provided the initiative petition is filed with the custodian of state records no later than February 1 of the year in which the general election is held.
(c) The legislature shall provide by general law, prior to the holding of an election pursuant to this section, for the provision of a statement to the public regarding the probable financial impact of any amendment proposed by initiative pursuant to section 3.
(d) Once in the tenth week, and once in the sixth week immediately preceding the week in which the election is held, the proposed amendment or revision, with notice of the date of election at which it will be submitted to the electors, shall be published in one newspaper of general circulation in each county in which a newspaper is published.
(e) Unless otherwise specifically provided for elsewhere in this constitution, if the proposed amendment or revision is approved by vote of at least sixty percent of the electors voting on the measure, it shall be effective as an amendment to or revision of the constitution of the state on the first Tuesday after the first Monday in January following the election, or on such other date as may be specified in the amendment or revision.

Section 6. Taxation and Budget Reform Commission

(a) Beginning in 2007 and each twentieth year thereafter, there shall be established a taxation and budget reform commission composed of the following members:

(1) eleven members selected by the governor, none of whom shall be a member of the legislature at the time of appointment.
(2) seven members selected by the speaker of the house of representatives and seven members selected by the president of the senate, none of whom shall be a member of the legislature at the time of appointment.
(3) four non-voting ex officio members, all of whom shall be members of the legislature at the time of appointment. Two of these members, one of whom shall be a member of the minority party in the house of representatives, shall be selected by the speaker of the house of representatives, and two of these members, one of whom shall be a member of the minority party in the senate, shall be selected by the president of the senate.

(b) Vacancies in the membership of the commission shall be filled in the same manner as the original appointments.
(c) At its initial meeting, the members of the commission shall elect a member who is not a member of the legislature to serve as chair and the commission shall adopt its rules of procedure. Thereafter, the commission shall convene at the call of the chair. An affirmative vote of two thirds of the full commission shall be necessary for any revision of this constitution or any part of it to be proposed by the commission.
(d) The commission shall examine the state budgetary process, the revenue needs and expenditure processes of the state, the appropriateness of the tax structure of the state, and governmental productivity and efficiency; review policy as it relates to the ability of state and local government to tax and adequately fund governmental operations and capital facilities required to meet the state's needs during the next twenty year period; determine methods favored by the citizens of the state to fund the needs of the state, including alternative methods for

raising sufficient revenues for the needs of the state; determine measures that could be instituted to effectively gather funds from existing tax sources; examine constitutional limitations on taxation and expenditures at the state and local level; and review the state's comprehensive planning, budgeting and needs assessment processes to determine whether the resulting information adequately supports a strategic decisionmaking process.

(e) The commission shall hold public hearings as it deems necessary to carry out its responsibilities under this section. The commission shall issue a report of the results of the review carried out, and propose to the legislature any recommended statutory changes related to the taxation or budgetary laws of the state. Not later than one hundred eighty days prior to the general election in the second year following the year in which the commission is established, the commission shall file with the custodian of state records its proposal, if any, of a revision of this constitution or any part of it dealing with taxation or the state budgetary process.

Section 7. Tax or Fee Limitation

Notwithstanding Article X, Section 12(d) of this constitution, no new State tax or fee shall be imposed on or after November 8, 1994 by any amendment to this constitution unless the proposed amendment is approved by not fewer than two-thirds of the voters voting in the election in which such proposed amendment is considered. For purposes of this section, the phrase "new State tax or fee" shall mean any tax or fee which would produce revenue subject to lump sum or other appropriation by the Legislature, either for the State general revenue fund or any trust fund, which tax or fee is not in effect on November 7, 1994 including without limitation such taxes and fees as are the subject of proposed constitutional amendments appearing on the ballot on November 8, 1994. This section shall apply to proposed constitutional amendments relating to State taxes or fees which appear on the November 8, 1994 ballot, or later ballots, and any such proposed amendment which fails to gain the two-thirds vote required hereby shall be null, void and without effect.

ARTICLE XII: SCHEDULE

Section 1. Constitution of 1885 superseded Articles I through IV, VII, and IX through XX of the Constitution of Florida adopted in 1885, as amended from time to time, are superseded by this revision except those sections expressly retained and made a part of this revision by reference.

Section 2. Property taxes; millages Tax millages authorized in counties, municipalities and special districts, on the date this revision becomes effective, may be continued until reduced by law.

Section 3. Officers to continue in office Every person holding office when this revision becomes effective shall continue in office for the remainder of the term if that office is not abolished. If the office is abolished the incumbent shall be paid adequate compensation, to be fixed by law, for the loss of emoluments for the remainder of the term.

Section 4. State commissioner of education The state superintendent of public instruction in office on the effective date of this revision shall become and, for the remainder of the term being served, shall be the commissioner of education.

Section 5. Superintendent of Schools

(a) On the effective date of this revision the county superintendent of public instruction of each county shall become and, for the remainder of the term being served, shall be the superintendent of schools of that district.
(b) The method of selection of the county superintendent of public instruction of each county, as provided by or under the Constitution of 1885, as amended, shall apply to the selection of the district superintendent of schools until changed as herein provided.

Section 6. Laws Preserved

(a) All laws in effect upon the adoption of this revision, to the extent not inconsistent with it, shall remain in force until they expire by their terms or are repealed.
(b) All statutes which, under the Constitution of 1885, as amended, apply to the state superintendent of public instruction and those which apply to the county superintendent of public instruction shall under this revision apply, respectively, to the state commissioner of education and the district superintendent of schools.

Section 7. Rights Reserved

(a) All actions, rights of action, claims, contracts and obligations of individuals, corporations and public bodies or agencies existing on the date this revision becomes effective shall continue to be valid as if this revision had not been adopted. All taxes, penalties, fines and forfeitures owing to the state under the Constitution of 1885, as amended, shall inure to the state under this revision, and all sentences as punishment for crime shall be executed according to their terms.
(b) This revision shall not be retroactive so as to create any right or liability which did not exist under the Constitution of 1885, as amended, based upon matters occurring prior to the adoption of this revision.

Section 8. Public debts recognized All bonds, revenue certificates, revenue bonds and tax anticipation certificates issued pursuant to the Constitution of 1885, as amended by the state, any agency, political subdivision or public corporation of the state shall remain in full force and effect and shall be secured by the same sources of revenue as before the adoption of this revision, and, to the extent necessary to effectuate this section, the applicable provisions of the Constitution of 1885, as amended, are retained as a part of this revision until payment in full of these public securities.

Section 9. Bonds

(a) Additional Securities.

(1) Article IX, Section 17, of the Constitution of 1885, as amended, as it existed immediately before this Constitution, as revised in 1968, became effective, is adopted by this reference as a part of this revision as completely as though incorporated herein verbatim, except revenue bonds, revenue certificates or other evidences of indebtedness hereafter issued thereunder may be issued by the agency of the state so authorized by law.
(2) That portion of Article XII, Section 9, Subsection (a) of this Constitution, as amended, which by reference adopted Article XII, Section 19 of the Constitution of 1885, as amended, as the same existed immediately before the effective date of this amendment is adopted by this reference as part of this revision as completely as though incorporated herein verbatim, for the purpose of providing that after the effective date of this amendment all of the proceeds of the revenues derived from the gross receipts taxes, as therein defined, collected in each year shall be applied as provided therein to the extent necessary to comply with all obligations to or for the benefit of holders of bonds or certificates issued before the effective date of this amendment or any refundings thereof which are secured by such gross receipts taxes. No bonds or other obligations may be issued pursuant to the provisions of Article XII, Section 19, of the Constitution of 1885, as amended, but this provision shall not be construed to prevent the refunding of any such outstanding bonds or obligations pursuant to the provisions of this subsection (a)(2).

Subject to the requirements of the first paragraph of this subsection (a)(2), beginning July 1, 1975, all of the proceeds of the revenues derived from the gross receipts taxes collected from every person, including municipalities, as provided and levied pursuant to the provisions of chapter 203, Florida Statutes, as such chapter is amended from time to time, shall, as collected, be placed in a trust fund to be known as the "public education capital outlay and debt service trust fund" in the state treasury (hereinafter referred to as "capital outlay fund"), and used only as provided herein.

The capital outlay fund shall be administered by the state board of education as created and constituted by Section 2 of Article IX of the Constitution of Florida as revised in 1968 (hereinafter referred to as "state board"), or by such other instrumentality of the state which shall hereafter succeed by law to the powers, duties and functions of the state board, including the powers, duties and functions of the state board provided in this subsection (a)(2). The state board shall be a body corporate and shall have all the powers provided herein in addition to all other constitutional and statutory powers related to the purposes of this subsection (a)(2) heretofore or hereafter conferred by law upon the state board, or its predecessor created by the Constitution of 1885, as amended.

State bonds pledging the full faith and credit of the state may be issued, without a vote of the electors, by the state board pursuant to law to finance or refinance capital projects theretofore authorized by the legislature, and any purposes appurtenant or incidental thereto, for the state system of public education provided for in Section 1 of Article IX of this Constitution (hereinafter referred to as "state system"), including but not limited to institutions of higher learning, community colleges, vocational technical schools, or public schools, as now defined or as may hereafter be defined by law. All such bonds shall mature not later than thirty years after the date of issuance thereof. All other details of such bonds shall be as provided by law or by the proceedings authorizing such bonds; provided, however, that no bonds, except refunding bonds, shall be issued, and no proceeds shall be expended for the cost of any capital project, unless such project has been authorized by the legislature.

Bonds issued pursuant to this subsection (a)(2) shall be primarily payable from such revenues derived from gross receipts taxes, and shall be additionally secured by the full faith and credit of the state. No such bonds shall ever be issued in an amount exceeding ninety percent of the amount which the state board determines can be serviced by the revenues derived from the gross receipts taxes accruing thereafter under the provisions of this subsection (a)(2), and such determination shall be conclusive.

The moneys in the capital outlay fund in each fiscal year shall be used only for the following purposes and in the following order of priority:

a. For the payment of the principal of and interest on any bonds due in such fiscal year;
b. For the deposit into any reserve funds provided for in the proceedings authorizing the issuance of bonds of any amounts required to be deposited in such reserve funds in such fiscal year;
c. For direct payment of the cost or any part of the cost of any capital project for the state system theretofore authorized by the legislature, or for the purchase or redemption of outstanding bonds in accordance with the provisions of the proceedings which authorized the issuance of such bonds, or for the purpose of maintaining, restoring, or repairing existing public educational facilities.

(b) Refunding Bonds.
Revenue bonds to finance the cost of state capital projects issued prior to the date this revision becomes effective, including projects of the Florida state turnpike authority or its successor but excluding all portions of the state highway system, may be refunded as provided by law without vote of the electors at a lower net average interest cost rate by the issuance of bonds maturing not later than the obligations refunded, secured by the same revenues only.

(c) Motor Vehicle Fuel Taxes.

(1) A state tax, designated "second gas tax," of two cents per gallon upon gasoline and other like products of petroleum and an equivalent tax upon other sources of energy used to propel motor vehicles as levied by Article IX, Section 16, of the Constitution of 1885, as amended, is hereby continued. The proceeds of said tax shall be placed monthly in the state roads distribution fund in the state treasury.

(2) Article IX, Section 16, of the Constitution of 1885, as amended, is adopted by this reference as a part of this revision as completely as though incorporated herein verbatim for the purpose of providing that after the effective date of this revision the proceeds of the "second gas tax" as referred to therein shall be allocated among the several counties in accordance with the formula stated therein to the extent necessary to comply with all obligations to or for the benefit of holders of bonds, revenue certificates and tax anticipation certificates or any refundings thereof secured by any portion of the "second gas tax."

(3) No funds anticipated to be allocated under the formula stated in Article IX, Section 16, of the Constitution of 1885, as amended, shall be pledged as security for any obligation hereafter issued or entered into, except that any outstanding obligations previously issued pledging revenues allocated under said Article IX, Section 16, may be refunded at a lower average net interest cost rate by the issuance of refunding bonds, maturing not later than the obligations refunded, secured by the same revenues and any other security authorized in paragraph (5) of this subsection.

(4) Subject to the requirements of paragraph (2) of this subsection and after payment of administrative expenses, the "second gas tax" shall be allocated to the account of each of the several counties in the amounts to be determined as follows: There shall be an initial allocation of one-fourth in the ratio of county area to state area, one-fourth in the ratio of the total county population to the total population of the state in accordance with the latest available federal census, and one-half in the ratio of the total "second gas tax" collected on retail sales or use in each county to the total collected in all counties of the state during the previous fiscal year. If the annual debt service requirements of any obligations issued for any county, including any deficiencies for prior years, secured under paragraph (2) of this subsection, exceeds the amount which would be allocated to that county under the formula set out in this paragraph, the amounts allocated to other counties shall be reduced proportionately.

(5) Funds allocated under paragraphs (2) and (4) of this subsection shall be administered by the state board of administration created under Article IV, Section 4. The board shall remit the proceeds of the "second gas tax" in each county account for use in said county as follows: eighty per cent to the state agency supervising the state road system and twenty per cent to the governing body of the county. The percentage allocated to the county may be increased by general law. The proceeds of the "second gas tax" subject to allocation to the several counties under this paragraph (5) shall be used first, for the payment of obligations pledging revenues allocated pursuant to Article IX, Section 16, of the Constitution of 1885, as amended, and any refundings thereof; second, for the payment of debt service on bonds issued as provided by this paragraph (5) to finance the acquisition and construction of roads as defined by law; and third, for the acquisition and construction of roads and for road maintenance as authorized by law. When authorized by law, state bonds pledging the full faith and credit of the state may be issued without any election: (i) to refund obligations secured by any portion of the "second gas tax" allocated to a county under Article IX, Section 16, of the Constitution of 1885, as amended; (ii) to finance the acquisition and construction of roads in a county when approved by the governing body of the county and the state agency supervising the state road system; and (iii) to refund obligations secured by any portion of the "second gas tax" allocated under paragraph 9(c)(4). No such bonds shall be issued unless a state fiscal agency created by law has made a determination that in no state fiscal year will the debt service requirements of the bonds and all other bonds secured by the pledged portion of the "second gas tax" allocated to the county exceed seventy-five per cent of the pledged portion of the "second gas tax" allocated to that county for the preceding state fiscal year, of the pledged net tolls from existing facilities collected in the preceding state fiscal year, and of the annual average net tolls anticipated during the first five state fiscal years of operation of new projects to be financed, and of any other legally available pledged revenues collected in the preceding state fiscal year. Bonds issued pursuant to this subsection shall be payable primarily from the pledged tolls, the pledged portions of the "second gas tax" allocated to that county, and any other pledged revenue, and shall mature not later than forty years from the date of issuance.

(d) School Bonds.

(1) Article XII, Section 9, Subsection (d) of this constitution, as amended, (which, by reference, adopted 6Article XII, Section 18, of the Constitution of 1885, as amended) as the same existed immediately before the effective date of this amendment is adopted by this reference as part of this amendment as completely as though incorporated herein verbatim, for the purpose of providing that after the effective date of this amendment the first proceeds of the revenues derived from the licensing of motor vehicles as referred to therein shall be distributed annually among the several counties in the ratio of the number of instruction units in each county, the same being coterminus with the school district of each county as provided in Article IX, Section 4, Subsection (a) of this constitution, in each year computed as provided therein to the extent necessary to comply with all obligations to or for the benefit of holders of bonds or motor vehicle tax anticipation certificates issued before the effective date of this amendment or any refundings thereof which are secured by any portion of such revenues derived from the licensing of motor vehicles.
(2) No funds anticipated to be distributed annually among the several counties under the formula stated in Article XII, Section 9, Subsection (d) of this constitution, as amended, as the same existed immediately before the effective date of this amendment

shall be pledged as security for any obligations hereafter issued or entered into, except that any outstanding obligations previously issued pledging such funds may be refunded by the issuance of refunding bonds.

(3) Subject to the requirements of paragraph (1) of this subsection (d) beginning July 1, 1973, the first proceeds of the revenues derived from the licensing of motor vehicles (hereinafter called "motor vehicle license revenues") to the extent necessary to comply with the provisions of this amendment, shall, as collected, be placed monthly in the school district and community college district capital outlay and debt service fund in the state treasury and used only as provided in this amendment. Such revenue shall be distributed annually among the several school districts and community college districts in the ratio of the number of instruction units in each school district or community college district in each year computed as provided herein. The amount of the first motor vehicle license revenues to be so set aside in each year and distributed as provided herein shall be an amount equal in the aggregate to the product of six hundred dollars ($600) multiplied by the total number of instruction units in all the school districts of Florida for the school fiscal year 1967-68, plus an amount equal in the aggregate to the product of eight hundred dollars ($800) multiplied by the total number of instruction units in all the school districts of Florida for the school fiscal year 1972-73 and for each school fiscal year thereafter which is in excess of the total number of such instruction units in all the school districts of Florida for the school fiscal year 1967-68, such excess units being designated "growth units." The amount of the first motor vehicle license revenues to be so set aside in each year and distributed as provided herein shall additionally be an amount equal in the aggregate to the product of four hundred dollars ($400) multiplied by the total number of instruction units in all community college districts of Florida. The number of instruction units in each school district or community college district in each year for the purposes of this amendment shall be the greater of (1) the number of instruction units in each school district for the school fiscal year 1967-68 or community college district for the school fiscal year 1968-69 computed in the manner heretofore provided by general law, or (2) the number of instruction units in such school district, including growth units, or community college district for the school fiscal year computed in the manner heretofore or hereafter provided by general law and approved by the state board of education (hereinafter called the state board), or (3) the number of instruction units in each school district, including growth units, or community college district on behalf of which the state board has issued bonds or motor vehicle license revenue anticipation certificates under this amendment which will produce sufficient revenues under this amendment to equal one and twelve-hundredths (1.12) times the aggregate amount of principal of and interest on all bonds or motor vehicle license revenue anticipation certificates issued under this amendment which will mature and become due in such year, computed in the manner heretofore or hereafter provided by general law and approved by the state board.

(4) Such funds so distributed shall be administered by the state board as now created and constituted by Section 2 of Article IX of the State Constitution as revised in 1968, or by such other instrumentality of the state which shall hereafter succeed by law to the powers, duties and functions of the state board, including the powers, duties and functions of the state board provided in this amendment. For the purposes of this amendment, said state board shall be a body corporate and shall have all the powers provided in this amendment in addition to all other constitutional and statutory powers related to the purposes of this amendment heretofore or hereafter conferred upon said state board.

(5) The state board shall, in addition to its other constitutional and statutory powers, have the management, control and supervision of the proceeds of the first motor vehicle license revenues provided for in this subsection (d). The state board shall also have power, for the purpose of obtaining funds for the use of any school board of any school district or board of trustees of any community college district in acquiring, building, constructing, altering, remodeling, improving, enlarging, furnishing, equipping, maintaining, renovating, or repairing of capital outlay projects for school purposes to issue bonds or motor vehicle license revenue anticipation certificates, and also to issue such bonds or motor vehicle license revenue anticipation certificates to pay, fund or refund any bonds or motor vehicle license revenue anticipation certificates theretofore issued by said state board. All such bonds or motor vehicle license revenue anticipation certificates shall bear interest at not exceeding the rate provided by general law and shall mature not later than thirty years after the date of issuance thereof. The state board shall have power to determine all other details of the bonds or motor vehicle license revenue anticipation certificates and to sell in the manner provided by general law, or exchange the bonds or motor vehicle license revenue anticipation certificates, upon such terms and conditions as the state board shall provide.

(6) The state board shall also have power to pledge for the payment of the principal of and interest on such bonds or motor vehicle license revenue anticipation certificates, including refunding bonds or refunding motor vehicle license revenue anticipation certificates, all or any part from the motor vehicle license revenues provided for in this amendment and to enter into any covenants and other agreements with the holders of such bonds or motor vehicle license revenue anticipation certificates at the time of the issuance thereof concerning the security thereof and the rights of the holders thereof, all of which covenants and agreements shall constitute legally binding and irrevocable contracts with such holders and shall be fully enforceable by such holders in any court of competent jurisdiction.

(7) No such bonds or motor vehicle license revenue anticipation certificates shall ever be issued by the state board, except to refund outstanding bonds or motor vehicle license revenue anticipation certificates, until after the adoption of a resolution requesting the issuance thereof by the school board of the school district or board of trustees of the community college district on behalf of which the obligations are to be issued. The state board of education shall limit the amount of such bonds or motor vehicle license revenue anticipation certificates which can be issued on behalf of any school district or community college district to ninety percent (90%) of the amount which it determines can be serviced by the revenue accruing to the school district or community college district under the provisions of this amendment, and shall determine the reasonable allocation of the interest savings from the issuance of refunding bonds or motor vehicle license revenue anticipation certificates, and such determinations shall be conclusive. All such bonds or motor vehicle license revenue anticipation certificates shall be issued in the name of the state board of education but shall be issued for and on behalf of the school board of the school district or board of trustees of the community college district requesting the issuance thereof, and no election or approval of qualified electors shall be required for the issuance thereof.

(8) The state board shall in each year use the funds distributable pursuant to this amendment to the credit of each school district or community college district only in the following manner and in order of priority:

a. To comply with the requirements of paragraph (1) of this subsection (d).

b. To pay all amounts of principal and interest due in such year on any bonds or motor vehicle license revenue anticipation certificates issued under the authority hereof, including refunding bonds or motor vehicle license revenue anticipation certificates, issued on behalf of the school board of such school district or board of trustees of such community college district; subject, however, to any covenants or agreements made by the state board concerning the rights between holders of different issues of such bonds or motor vehicle license revenue anticipation certificates, as herein authorized.

c. To establish and maintain a sinking fund or funds to meet future requirements for debt service or reserves therefor, on bonds or motor vehicle license revenue anticipation certificates issued on behalf of the school board of such school district or board of trustees of such community college district under the authority hereof, whenever the state board shall deem it necessary or advisable, and in such amounts and under such terms and conditions as the state board shall in its discretion determine.

d. To distribute annually to the several school boards of the school districts or the boards of trustees of the community college districts for use in payment of debt service on bonds heretofore or hereafter issued by any such school boards of the school districts or boards of trustees of the community college districts where the proceeds of the bonds were used, or are to be used, in the acquiring, building, constructing, altering, remodeling, improving, enlarging, furnishing, equipping, maintaining, renovating, or repairing of capital outlay projects in such school districts or community college districts and which capital outlay projects have been approved by the school board of the school district or board of trustees of the community college district, pursuant to the most recent survey or surveys conducted under regulations prescribed by the state board to determine the capital outlay needs of the school district or community college district. The state board shall have power at the time of issuance of any bonds by any school board of any school district or board of trustees of any community college district to covenant and agree with such school board or board of trustees as to the rank and priority of payments to be made for different issues of bonds under this subparagraph d., and may further agree that any amounts to be distributed under this subparagraph d. may be pledged for the debt service on bonds issued by any school board of any school district or board of trustees of any community college district and for the rank and priority of such pledge. Any such covenants or agreements of the state board may be enforced by any holders of such bonds in any court of competent jurisdiction.
e. To pay the expenses of the state board in administering this subsection (d), which shall be prorated among the various school districts and community college districts and paid out of the proceeds of the bonds or motor vehicle license revenue anticipation certificates or from the funds distributable to each school district and community college district on the same basis as such motor vehicle license revenues are distributable to the various school districts and community college districts.
f. To distribute annually to the several school boards of the school districts or boards of trustees of the community college

districts for the payment of the cost of acquiring, building, constructing, altering, remodeling, improving, enlarging, furnishing, equipping, maintaining, renovating, or repairing of capital outlay projects for school purposes in such school district or community college district as shall be requested by resolution of the school board of the school district or board of trustees of the community college district.

g. When all major capital outlay needs of a school district or community college district have been met as determined by the state board, on the basis of a survey made pursuant to regulations of the state board and approved by the state board, all such funds remaining shall be distributed annually and used for such school purposes in such school district or community college district as the school board of the school district or board of trustees of the community college district shall determine, or as may be provided by general law.

(9) Capital outlay projects of a school district or community college district shall be eligible to participate in the funds accruing under this amendment and derived from the proceeds of bonds and motor vehicle license revenue anticipation certificates and from the motor vehicle license revenues, only in the order of priority of needs, as shown by a survey or surveys conducted in the school district or community college district under regulations prescribed by the state board, to determine the capital outlay needs of the school district or community college district and approved by the state board; provided that the priority of such projects may be changed from time to time upon the request of the school board of the school district or board of trustees of the community college district and with the approval of the state board; and provided, further, that this paragraph (9) shall not in any manner affect any covenant, agreement or pledge made by the state board in the issuance by said state board of any bonds or motor vehicle license revenue anticipation certificates, or in connection with the issuance of any bonds of any school board of any school district or board of trustees of any community college district.

(10) The state board shall have power to make and enforce all rules and regulations necessary to the full exercise of the powers herein granted and no legislation shall be required to render this amendment of full force and operating effect. The legislature shall not reduce the levies of said motor vehicle license revenues during the life of this amendment to any degree which will fail to provide the full amount necessary to comply with the provisions of this amendment and pay the necessary expenses of administering the laws relating to the licensing of motor vehicles, and shall not enact any law having the effect of withdrawing the proceeds of such motor vehicle license revenues from the operation of this amendment and shall not enact any law impairing or materially altering the rights of the holders of any bonds or motor vehicle license revenue anticipation certificates issued pursuant to this amendment or impairing or altering any covenant or agreement of the state board, as provided in such bonds or motor vehicle license revenue anticipation certificates.

(11) Bonds issued by the state board pursuant to this subsection (d) shall be payable primarily from said motor vehicle license revenues as provided herein, and if heretofore or hereafter authorized by law, may be additionally secured by pledging the full faith and credit of the state without an election. When heretofore or hereafter authorized by law, bonds issued pursuant to Article XII, Section 18 of the Constitution of 1885, as amended prior to 1968, and bonds issued pursuant to Article XII, Section 9, subsection (d) of the Constitution as revised in 1968, and bonds issued pursuant to this subsection (d), may be refunded by the issuance of bonds additionally secured by the full faith and credit of the state.

(e) Debt Limitation.
Bonds issued pursuant to this Section 9 of Article XII which are payable primarily from revenues pledged pursuant to this section shall not be included in applying the limits upon the amount of state bonds contained in Section 11, Article VII, of this revision.

Section 17. Bonds; Land Acquisition for Outdoor Recreation Development

The outdoor recreational development council, as created by the 1963 legislature, may issue revenue bonds, revenue certificates or other evidences of indebtedness to acquire lands, water areas and related resources and to construct, improve, enlarge and extend capital improvements and facilities thereon in furtherance of outdoor recreation, natural resources conservation and related facilities in this state; provided, however, the legislature with respect to such revenue bonds, revenue certificates or other evidences of indebtedness shall designate the revenue or tax sources to be deposited in or credited to the land acquisition trust fund for their repayment and may impose restrictions on their issuance, including the fixing of maximum interest rates and discounts.

The land acquisition trust fund, created by the 1963 legislature for these multiple public purposes, shall continue from the date of the adoption of this amendment for a period of fifty years. In the event the outdoor recreational development council shall determine to issue bonds for financing acquisition of sites for multiple purposes the state board of administration shall act as fiscal agent, and the attorney general shall handle the validation proceedings.

All bonds issued under this amendment shall be sold at public sale after public advertisement upon such terms and conditions as the outdoor recreational development council shall provide and as otherwise provided by law and subject to the limitations herein imposed.

Section 19. Institutions of Higher Learning and Junior College Capital Outlay Trust Fund Bonds

(a) That beginning January 1, 1964, and for fifty years thereafter, all of the proceeds of the revenues derived from the gross receipts taxes collected from every person, including municipalities, receiving payment for electricity for light, heat or power, for natural or manufactured gas for light, heat or power, for use of telephones and for the sending of telegrams and telegraph messages, as now provided and levied as of the time of adoption of this amendment in Chapter 203, Florida Statutes (hereinafter called "Gross Receipts Taxes"), shall, as collected be placed in a trust fund to be known as the "Institutions of Higher Learning and Junior Colleges Capital Outlay and Debt Service Trust Fund" in the State Treasury (hereinafter referred to as "Capital Outlay Fund"), and used only as provided in this Amendment.

Said fund shall be administered by the State Board of Education, as now created and constituted by Section 3 of Article XII [now s. 2, Article IX] of the Constitution of Florida (hereinafter referred to as "State Board"). For the purpose of this Amendment, said State Board, as now constituted, shall continue as a body corporate during the life of this Amendment and shall have all the powers provided in this Amendment in addition to all other constitutional and statutory powers related to the purposes of this Amendment heretofore or hereafter conferred by law upon said State Board.

(b) The State Board shall have power, for the purpose of obtaining funds for acquiring, building, constructing, altering, improving, enlarging, furnishing or equipping capital outlay projects theretofore authorized by the legislature and any purposes appurtenant or incidental thereto, for Institutions of Higher Learning or Junior Colleges, as now defined or as may be hereafter defined by law, and for the purpose of constructing buildings and other permanent facilities for vocational technical schools as provided in chapter 230 Florida Statutes, to issue bonds or certificates, including refunding bonds or certificates to fund or refund any bonds or certificates theretofore issued. All such bonds or certificates shall bear interest at not exceeding four and one-half per centum per annum, and shall mature at such time or times as the State Board shall determine not exceeding, in any event, however, thirty years from the date of issuance thereof. The State Board shall have power to determine all other details of such bonds or certificates and to sell at public sale, after public advertisement, such bonds or certificates, provided, however, that no bonds or certificates shall ever be issued hereunder to finance, or the proceeds thereof expended for, any part of the cost of any capital outlay project unless the construction or acquisition of such capital outlay project has been theretofore authorized by the Legislature of Florida. None of said bonds or certificates shall be sold at less than ninety-eight per centum of the par value thereof, plus accrued interest, and said bonds or certificates shall be awarded at the public sale thereof to the bidder offering the lowest net interest cost for such bonds or certificates in the manner to be determined by the State Board.

The State Board shall also have power to pledge for the payment of the principal of and interest on such bonds or certificates, and reserves therefor, including refunding bonds or certificates, all or any part of the revenue to be derived from the said Gross Receipts Taxes provided for in this Amendment, and to enter into any covenants and other agreements with the holders of such bonds or certificates concerning the security thereof and the rights of the holders thereof, all of which covenants and agreements shall constitute legally binding and irrevocable contracts with such holders and shall be fully enforceable by such holders in any court of competent jurisdiction.

No such bonds or certificates shall ever be issued by the State Board in an amount exceeding seventy-five per centum of the amount which it determines, based upon the average annual amount of the revenues derived from said Gross Receipts Taxes during the immediately preceding two fiscal years, or the amount of the revenues derived from said Gross Receipts Taxes during the immediately preceding fiscal year, as shown in a certificate filed by the State Comptroller with the State Board prior to the issuance of such bonds or certificates, whichever is the lesser, can be serviced by the revenues accruing thereafter under the provisions of this Amendment; nor shall the State Board, during the first year following the ratification of this amendment, issue bonds or certificates in excess of seven times the anticipated revenue from said Gross Receipts Taxes during said year, nor during each succeeding year, more than four times the anticipated revenue from said Gross Receipts Taxes during such year. No election or approval of qualified electors or freeholder electors shall be required for the issuance of bonds or certificates hereunder.

After the initial issuance of any bonds or certificates pursuant to this Amendment, the State Board may thereafter issue additional bonds or certificates which will rank equally and on a parity, as to lien on and source of security for payment from said Gross Receipts Taxes, with any bonds or certificates theretofore issued pursuant to this Amendment, but such additional parity bonds or certificates shall not be issued unless the average annual amount of the revenues derived from said Gross Receipts Taxes during the immediately preceding two fiscal years, or the amount of the revenues derived from said Gross Receipts Taxes during the immediately preceding fiscal year, as shown in a certificate filed by the State Comptroller with the State Board prior to the issuance of such bonds or certificates, whichever is the lesser, shall have been equal to one and one-third times the aggregate amount of principal and interest which will become due in any succeeding fiscal year on all bonds or certificates theretofore issued pursuant to this Amendment and then outstanding, and the additional parity bonds or certificates then proposed to be issued. No bonds, certificates or other obligations whatsoever shall at any time be issued under the provisions of this

Amendment, except such bonds or certificates initially issued hereunder, and such additional parity bonds or certificates as provided in this paragraph. Notwithstanding any other provision herein no such bonds or certificates shall be authorized or validated during any biennium in excess of fifty million dollars, except by two-thirds vote of the members elected to each house of the legislature; provided further that during the biennium 1963-1965 seventy-five million dollars may be authorized and validated pursuant hereto.

(c) Capital outlay projects theretofore authorized by the legislature for any Institution of Higher Learning or Junior College shall be eligible to participate in the funds accruing under this Amendment derived from the proceeds of bonds or certificates and said Gross Receipts Taxes under such regulations and in such manner as shall be determined by the State Board, and the State Board shall use or transmit to the State Board of Control or to the Board of Public Instruction of any County authorized by law to construct or acquire such capital outlay projects, the amount of the proceeds of such bonds or certificates or Gross Receipts Taxes to be applied to or used for such capital outlay projects. If for any reason any of the proceeds of any bonds or certificates issued for any capital outlay project shall not be expended for such capital outlay project, the State Board may use such unexpended proceeds for any other capital outlay project for Institutions of Higher Learning or Junior Colleges and vocational technical schools, as defined herein, as now defined or as may be hereafter defined by law, theretofore authorized by the State Legislature. The holders of bonds or certificates issued hereunder shall not have any responsibility whatsoever for the application or use of any of the proceeds derived from the sale of said bonds or certificates, and the rights and remedies of the holders of such bonds or certificates and their right to payment from said Gross Receipts Taxes in the manner provided herein shall not be affected or impaired by the application or use of such proceeds.

The State Board shall use the moneys in said Capital Outlay Fund in each fiscal year only for the following purposes and in the following order of priority:

(1) For the payment of the principal of and interest on any bonds or certificates maturing in such fiscal year.
(2) For the deposit into any reserve funds provided for in the proceedings authorizing the issuance of said bonds or certificates, of any amounts required to be deposited in such reserve funds in such fiscal year.
(3) After all payments required in such fiscal year for the

purposes provided for in (1) and (2) above, including any deficiencies for required payments in prior fiscal years, any moneys remaining in said Capital Outlay Fund at the end of such fiscal year may be used by the State Board for direct payment of the cost or any part of the cost of any capital outlay project theretofore authorized by the legislature or for the purchase of any bonds or certificates issued hereunder then outstanding upon such terms and conditions as the State Board shall deem proper, or for the prior redemption of outstanding bonds or certificates in accordance with the provisions of the proceedings which authorized the issuance of such bonds or certificates. The State Board may invest the moneys in said Capital Outlay Fund or in any sinking fund or other funds created for any issue of bonds or certificates, in direct obligations of the United States of America or in the other securities referred to in Section 344.27, Florida Statutes.

(d) The State Board shall have the power to make and enforce all rules and regulations necessary to the full exercise of the powers herein granted and no legislation shall be required to render this Amendment of full force and operating effect on and after January 1, 1964. The Legislature, during the period this Amendment is in effect, shall not reduce the rate of said Gross Receipts Taxes now provided in said Chapter 203, Florida Statutes, or eliminate, exempt or remove any of the persons, firms or corporations, including municipal corporations, or any of the utilities, businesses or services now or hereafter subject to said Gross Receipts Taxes, from the levy and collection of said Gross Receipts Taxes as now provided in said Chapter 203, Florida Statutes, and shall not enact any law impairing or materially altering the rights of the holders of any bonds or certificates issued pursuant to this Amendment or impairing or altering any covenants or agreements of the State Board made hereunder, or having the effect of withdrawing the proceeds of said Gross Receipts Taxes from the operation of this Amendment. The State Board of Administration shall be and is hereby constituted as the Fiscal Agent of the State Board to perform such duties and assume such responsibilities under this

Amendment as shall be agreed upon between the State Board and such State Board of Administration. The State Board shall also have power to appoint such other persons and fix their compensation for the administration of the provisions of this Amendment as it shall deem necessary, and the expenses of the State Board in administering the provisions of this Amendment shall be paid out of the proceeds of bonds or certificates issued hereunder or from said Gross Receipts Taxes deposited in said Capital Outlay Fund.

(e) No capital outlay project or any part thereof shall be financed hereunder unless the bill authorizing such project shall specify it is financed hereunder and shall be approved by a vote of three-fifths of the elected members of each house.

Section 16. Board of Administration; Gasoline and Like Taxes, Distribution and Use; Etc

(a) That beginning January 1st, 1943, and for fifty (50) years thereafter, the proceeds of two (2¢) cents per gallon of the total tax levied by state law upon gasoline and other like products of petroleum, now known as the Second Gas Tax, and upon other fuels used to propel motor vehicles, shall as collected be placed monthly in the 'State Roads Distribution Fund' in the State Treasury and divided into three (3) equal parts which shall be distributed monthly among the several counties as follows: one part according to area, one part according to population, and one part according to the counties' contributions to the cost of state road construction in the ratio of distribution as provided in Chapter 15659, Laws of Florida, Acts of 1931, and for the purposes of the apportionment based on the counties' contributions for the cost of state road construction, the amount of the contributions established by the certificates made in 1931 pursuant to said Chapter 15659, shall be taken and deemed conclusive in computing the monthly amounts distributable according to said contributions. Such funds so distributed shall be administered by the State Board of Administration as hereinafter provided.

(b) The Governor as chairman, the State Treasurer, and the State Comptroller shall constitute a body corporate to be known as the 'State Board of Administration,' which board shall succeed to all the power, control and authority of the statutory Board of Administration. Said Board shall have, in addition to such powers as may be conferred upon it by law, the management, control and supervision of the proceeds of said two (2¢) cents of said taxes and all moneys and other assets which on the effective date of this amendment are applicable or may become applicable to the bonds of the several counties of this state, or any special road and bridge district, or other special taxing district thereof, issued prior to July 1st, 1931, for road and bridge purposes. The word 'bonds' as used herein shall include bonds, time warrants, notes and other forms of indebtedness issued for road and bridge purposes by any county or special road and bridge district or other special taxing district, outstanding on July 1st, 1931, or any refunding issues thereof. Said Board shall have the statutory powers of Boards of County Commissioners and Bond Trustees and of any other authority of special road and bridge districts, and other special taxing districts thereof with regard to said bonds, (except that the power to levy ad valorem taxes is expressly withheld from said Board), and shall take over all papers, documents and records concerning the same. Said Board shall have the power from time to time to issue refunding bonds to mature within the said fifty (50) year period, for any of said outstanding bonds or interest thereon, and to secure them by a pledge of anticipated receipts from such gasoline or other fuel taxes to be distributed to such county as herein provided, but not at a greater rate of interest than said bonds now bear; and to issue, sell or exchange on behalf of any county or unit for the sole purpose of retiring said bonds issued by such county, or special road and bridge district, or other special taxing district thereof, gasoline or other fuel tax anticipation certificates bearing interest at not more than three (3) per cent per annum in such denominations and maturing at such time within the fifty (50) year period as the board may determine. In addition to exercising the powers now provided by statute for the investment of sinking funds, said Board may use the sinking funds created for said bonds of any county or special road and bridge district, or other unit hereunder, to purchase the matured or maturing bonds participating herein of any other county or any other special road and bridge district, or other special taxing district thereof, provided that as to said matured bonds, the value thereof as an investment shall be the price paid therefor, which shall not exceed the par value plus accrued interest, and that said investment shall bear interest at the rate of three (3) per cent per annum.

(c) The said board shall annually use said funds in each county account, first, to pay current principal and interest maturing, if any, of said bonds and gasoline or other fuel tax anticipation certificates of such county or special road and bridge district, or other special taxing district thereof; second, to establish a sinking fund account to meet future requirements of said bonds and gasoline or other fuel tax anticipation certificates where it appears the anticipated income for any year or years will not equal scheduled payments thereon; and third, any remaining balance out of the proceeds of said two (2¢) cents of said taxes shall monthly during the year be remitted by said board as follows: Eighty (80%) per cent to the State Road Department for the construction or reconstruction of state roads and bridges within the county, or for the lease or purchase of bridges connecting state highways within the county, and twenty (20%) per cent to the Board of County Commissioners of such county for use on roads and bridges therein.

(d) Said board shall have the power to make and enforce all rules and regulations necessary to the full exercise of the powers hereby granted and no legislation shall be required to render this amendment of full force and operating effect from and after January 1st, 1943. The Legislature shall continue the levies of said taxes during the life of this Amendment, and shall not enact any law having the effect of withdrawing the proceeds of said two (2¢) cents of said taxes from the operation of this amendment. The board shall pay refunding expenses and other expenses for services rendered specifically for, or which are properly chargeable to, the account of any county from funds distributed to such county; but general expenses of the board for services rendered all the counties alike shall be prorated among them and paid out of said funds on the same basis said tax proceeds are distributed among the several counties; provided, report of said expenses shall be made to each Regular Session of the Legislature, and the Legislature may limit the expenses of the board.

Section 18. School Bonds for Capital Outlay, Issuance

(a) Beginning January 1, 1965 and for thirty-five years thereafter, the first proceeds of the revenues derived from the licensing of motor vehicles to the extent necessary to comply with the provisions of this amendment, shall, as collected, be placed monthly in the county capital outlay and debt service school fund in the state treasury, and used only as provided in this amendment. Such revenue shall be distributed annually among the several counties in the ratio of the number of instruction units in each county in each year computed as provided herein. The amount of the first revenues derived from the licensing of motor vehicles to be so set aside in each year and distributed as provided herein shall be an amount equal in the aggregate to the product of four hundred dollars multiplied by the total number of instruction units in all the counties of Florida. The number of instruction units in each county in each year for the purposes of this amendment shall be the greater of (1) the number of instruction units in each county for the school fiscal year 1951-52 computed in the manner heretofore provided by general law, or (2) the number of instruction units in such county for the school fiscal year computed in the manner heretofore or hereafter provided by general law and approved by the state board of education (hereinafter called the state board), or (3) the number of instruction units in each county on behalf of which the state board of education has issued bonds or motor vehicle tax anticipation certificates under this amendment which will produce sufficient revenues under this amendment to equal one and one-third times the aggregate amount of principal of and interest on such bonds or motor vehicle tax anticipation certificates which will mature and become due in such year, computed in the manner heretofore or hereafter provided by general law and approved by the state board.

Such funds so distributed shall be administered by the state board as now created and constituted by Section 3 of Article XII [now s. 2, Article IX] of the Constitution of Florida. For the purposes of this amendment, said state board, as now constituted, shall continue as a body corporate during the life of this amendment and shall have all the powers provided in this amendment in addition to all other constitutional and statutory powers related to the purposes of this amendment heretofore or hereafter conferred upon said board.

(b) The state board shall, in addition to its other constitutional and statutory powers, have the management, control and supervision of the proceeds of the first part of the revenues derived from the licensing of motor vehicles provided for in subsection (a). The state board shall also have power, for the purpose of obtaining funds for the use of any county board of public instruction in acquiring, building, constructing, altering, improving, enlarging, furnishing, or equipping capital outlay projects for school purposes, to issue bonds or motor vehicle tax anticipation certificates, and also to issue such bonds or motor vehicle tax anticipation certificates to pay, fund or refund any bonds or motor vehicle tax anticipation certificates theretofore issued by said state board. All such bonds shall bear interest at not exceeding four and one-half per centum per annum and shall mature serially in annual installments commencing not more than three years from the date of issuance thereof and ending not later than thirty years from the date of issuance or January 1, 2000, A.D., whichever is earlier. All such motor vehicle tax anticipation certificates shall bear interest at not exceeding four and one-half per centum per annum and shall mature prior to January 1, 2000, A.D. The state board shall have power to determine all other details of said bonds or motor vehicle tax anticipation certificates and to sell at public sale after public advertisement, or exchange said bonds or motor vehicle tax anticipation certificates, upon such terms and conditions as the state board shall provide.

The state board shall also have power to pledge for the payment of the principal of and interest on such bonds or motor vehicle tax anticipation certificates, including refunding bonds or refunding motor vehicle tax anticipation certificates, all or any part from the anticipated revenues to be derived from the licensing of motor vehicles provided for in this amendment and to enter into any covenants and other agreements with the holders of such bonds or motor vehicle tax anticipation certificates at the time of the issuance thereof concerning the security thereof and the rights of the holders thereof, all of which covenants and agreements shall constitute legally binding and irrevocable contracts with such holders and shall be fully enforceable by such holders in any court of competent jurisdiction.

No such bonds or motor vehicle tax anticipation certificates shall ever be issued by the state board until after the adoption of a resolution requesting the issuance thereof by the county board of public instruction of the county on behalf of which such obligations are to be issued. The state board of education shall limit the amount of such bonds or motor vehicle tax anticipation certificates which can be issued on behalf of any county to seventy-five per cent of the amount which it determines can be serviced by the revenue accruing to the county under the provisions of this amendment, and such determination shall be conclusive. All such bonds or motor vehicle tax anticipation certificates shall be issued in the name of the state board of education but shall be issued for and on behalf of the county board of public instruction requesting the issuance thereof, and no election or approval of qualified electors or freeholders shall be required for the issuance thereof.

(c) The State Board shall in each year use the funds distributable pursuant to this Amendment to the credit of each county only in the following manner and order of priority:

(1) To pay all amounts of principal and interest maturing in such year on any bonds or motor vehicle tax anticipation certificates issued under the authority hereof, including refunding bonds or motor vehicle tax anticipation certificates, issued on behalf of the Board of Public Instruction of such county; subject, however, to any covenants or agreements made by the State Board concerning the rights between holders of different issues of such bonds or motor vehicle tax anticipation certificates, as herein authorized.
(2) To establish and maintain a sinking fund or funds to meet future requirements for debt service, or reserves therefor, on bonds or motor vehicle tax anticipation certificates issued on behalf of the Board of Public Instruction of such county, under the authority hereof, whenever the State Board shall deem it necessary or advisable, and in such amounts and under such terms and conditions as the State Board shall in its discretion determine.
(3) To distribute annually to the several Boards of Public Instruction of the counties for use in payment of debt service on bonds heretofore or hereafter issued by any such Board where the proceeds of the bonds were used, or are to be used, in the construction, acquisition, improvement, enlargement, furnishing, or equipping of capital outlay projects in such county, and which capital outlay projects have been approved by the Board of Public Instruction of the county, pursuant to a survey or surveys conducted subsequent to July 1, 1947 in the county, under regulations prescribed by the State Board to determine the capital outlay needs of the county.

The State Board shall have power at the time of issuance of any bonds by any Board of Public Instruction to covenant and agree with such Board as to the rank and priority of payments to be made for different issues of bonds under this Subsection (3), and may further agree that any amounts to be distributed under this Subsection (3) may be pledged for the debt service on bonds issued by any Board of Public Instruction and for the rank and priority of such pledge. Any such covenants or agreements of the State Board may be enforced by any holders of such bonds in any court of competent jurisdiction.

(4) To distribute annually to the several Boards of Public Instruction of the counties for the payment of the cost of the construction, acquisition, improvement, enlargement, furnishing, or equipping of capital outlay projects for school purposes in such county as shall be requested by resolution of the County Board of Public Instruction of such county.

(5) When all major capital outlay needs of a county have been met as determined by the State Board, on the basis of a survey made pursuant to regulations of the State Board and approved by the State Board, all such funds remaining shall be distributed annually and used for such school purposes in such county as the Board of Public Instruction of the county shall determine, or as may be provided by general law.

(d) Capital outlay projects of a county shall be eligible to participate in the funds accruing under this Amendment and derived from the proceeds of bonds and motor vehicle tax anticipation certificates and from the motor vehicle license taxes, only in the order of priority of needs, as shown by a survey or surveys conducted in the county under regulations prescribed by the State Board, to determine the capital outlay needs of the county and approved by the State Board; provided, that the priority of such projects may be changed from time to time upon the request of the Board of Public Instruction of the county and with the approval of the State Board; and provided further, that this Subsection (d) shall not in any manner affect any covenant, agreement, or pledge made by the State Board in the issuance by said State Board of any bonds or motor vehicle tax anticipation certificates, or in connection with the issuance of any bonds of any Board of Public Instruction of any county.

(e) The State Board may invest any sinking fund or funds created pursuant to this Amendment in direct obligations of the United States of America or in the bonds or motor vehicle tax anticipation certificates, matured or to mature, issued by the State Board on behalf of the Board of Public Instruction of any county.

(f) The State Board shall have power to make and enforce all rules and regulations necessary to the full exercise of the powers herein granted and no legislation shall be required to render this Amendment of full force and operating effect from and after January 1, 1953. The Legislature shall not reduce the levies of said motor vehicle license taxes during the life of this Amendment to any degree which will fail to provide the full amount necessary to comply with the provisions of this Amendment and pay the necessary expenses of administering the laws relating to the licensing of motor vehicles, and shall not enact any law having the effect of withdrawing the proceeds of such motor vehicle license taxes from the operation of this Amendment and shall not enact any law impairing or materially altering the rights of the holders of any bonds or motor vehicle tax anticipation certificates issued pursuant to this Amendment or impairing or altering any covenant or agreement of the State Board, as provided in such bonds or motor vehicle tax anticipation certificates.

The State Board shall have power to appoint such persons and fix their compensation for the administration of the provisions of this Amendment as it shall deem necessary, and the expenses of the State Board in administering the provisions of this Amendment shall be prorated among the various counties and paid out of the proceeds of the bonds or motor vehicle tax anticipation certificates or from the funds distributable to each county on the same basis as such motor vehicle license taxes are distributable to the various counties under the provisions of this Amendment. Interest or profit on sinking fund investments shall accrue to the counties in proportion to their respective equities in the sinking fund or funds.

Section 10. Preservation of Existing Government
All provisions of Articles I through IV, VII and IX through XX of the Constitution of 1885, as amended, not embraced herein which are not inconsistent with this revision shall become statutes subject to modification or repeal as are other statutes.

Section 11. Deletion of Obsolete Schedule Items
The legislature shall have power, by joint resolution, to delete from this revision any section of this Article XII, including this section, when all events to which the section to be deleted is or could become applicable have occurred. A legislative determination of fact made as a basis for application of this section shall be subject to judicial review.

Section 12. Senators
The requirements of staggered terms of senators in Section 15(a), of Article III of this revision shall apply only to senators elected in November, 1972, and thereafter.

Section 13. Legislative Apportionment
The requirements of legislative apportionment in Section 16 of Article III of this revision shall apply only to the apportionment of the legislature following the decennial census of 1970, and thereafter.

Section 14. Representatives; Terms
The legislature at its first regular session following the ratification of this revision, by joint resolution, shall propose to the electors of the state for ratification or rejection in the general election of 1970 an amendment to Article III, Section 15(b), of the constitution providing staggered terms of four years for members of the house of representatives.

Section 15. Special District Taxes
Ad valorem taxing power vested by law in special districts existing when this revision becomes effective shall not be abrogated by Section 9(b) of Article VII herein, but such powers, except to the extent necessary to pay outstanding debts, may be restricted or withdrawn by law.

Section 16. Reorganization
The requirement of Section 6, Article IV of this revision shall not apply until July 1, 1969.

Section 17. Conflicting Provisions

This schedule is designed to effect the orderly transition of government from the Constitution of 1885, as amended, to this revision and shall control in all cases of conflict with any part of Article I through IV, VII, and IX through XI herein.

Section 18. Bonds for Housing and Related Facilities

Section 16 of Article VII, providing for bonds for housing and related facilities, shall take effect upon approval by the electors.

Section 19. Renewable Energy Source Property

The amendment to Section 3 of Article VII, relating to an exemption for a renewable energy source device and real property on which such device is installed, if adopted at the special election in October 1980, shall take effect January 1, 1981.

Section 20. Access to Public Records

Section 24 of Article I, relating to access to public records, shall take effect July 1, 1993.

Section 21. State Revenue Limitation

The amendment to Section 1 of Article VII limiting state revenues shall take effect January 1, 1995, and shall first be applicable to state fiscal year 1995-1996.

Section 22. Historic Property Exemption and Assessment

The amendments to Sections 3 and 4 of Article VII relating to ad valorem tax exemption for, and assessment of, historic property shall take effect January 1, 1999.

Section 23. Fish and Wildlife Conservation Commission

(a) The initial members of the commission shall be the members of the game and fresh water fish commission and the marine fisheries commission who are serving on those commissions on the effective date of this amendment, who may serve the remainder of their respective terms. New appointments to the commission shall not be made until the retirement, resignation, removal, or expiration of the terms of the initial members results in fewer than seven members remaining.

(b) The jurisdiction of the marine fisheries commission as set forth in statutes in effect on March 1, 1998, shall be transferred to the fish and wildlife conservation commission. The jurisdiction of the marine fisheries commission transferred to the commission shall not be expanded except as provided by general law. All rules of the marine fisheries commission and game and fresh water fish commission in effect on the effective date of this amendment shall become rules of the fish and wildlife conservation commission until superseded or amended by the commission.

(c) On the effective date of this amendment, the marine fisheries commission and game and fresh water fish commission shall be abolished.

(d) This amendment shall take effect July 1, 1999.

Section 24. Executive Branch Reform

(a) The amendments contained in this revision shall take effect January 7, 2003, but shall govern with respect to the qualifying for and the holding of primary elections in 2002. The office of chief financial officer shall be a new office as a result of this revision.

(b) In the event the secretary of state is removed as a cabinet office in the 1998 general election, the term "custodian of state records" shall be substituted for the term "secretary of state" throughout the constitution and the duties previously performed by the secretary of state shall be as provided by law.

Section 25. Schedule to Article V Amendment

(a) Commencing with fiscal year 2000-2001, the legislature shall appropriate funds to pay for the salaries, costs, and expenses set forth in the amendment to Section 14 of Article V pursuant to a phase-in schedule established by general law.

(b) Unless otherwise provided herein, the amendment to Section 14 shall be fully effectuated by July 1, 2004.

Section 26. Increased Homestead Exemption

The amendment to Section 6 of Article VII increasing the maximum additional amount of the homestead exemption for low-income seniors shall take effect January 1, 2007.

Section 27. Property Tax Exemptions and Limitations on Property Tax Assessments

The amendments to Sections 3, 4, and 6 of Article VII, providing a $25,000 exemption for tangible personal property, providing an additional $25,000 homestead exemption, authorizing transfer of the accrued benefit from the limitations on the assessment of homestead property, and this section, if submitted to the electors of this state for approval or rejection at a special election authorized by law to be held on January 29, 2008, shall take effect upon approval by the electors and shall operate retroactively to January 1, 2008, or, if submitted to the electors of this state for approval or rejection at the next general election, shall take effect January 1 of the year following such general election. The amendments to Section 4 of Article VII creating subsections (f) and (g) of that section, creating a limitation on annual assessment increases for specified real property, shall take effect upon approval of the electors and shall first limit assessments beginning January 1, 2009, if approved at a special election held on January 29, 2008, or shall first limit assessments beginning January 1, 2010, if approved at the general election held in November of 2008. Subsections (f) and (g) of Section 4 of Article VII are repealed effective January 1, 2019; however, the legislature shall by joint resolution propose an amendment abrogating the repeal of subsections (f) and (g), which shall be submitted to the electors of this state for approval or rejection at the general election of 2018 and, if approved, shall take effect January 1, 2019.

Section 28. Property Tax Exemption and Classification and Assessment of Land Used for Conservation Purposes

The amendment to Section 3 of Article VII requiring the creation of an ad valorem tax exemption for real property dedicated in perpetuity for conservation purposes, and the amendment to Section 4 of Article VII requiring land used for conservation purposes to be classified by general law and assessed solely on the basis of character or use for purposes of ad valorem taxation, shall take effect upon approval by the electors and shall be implemented by January 1, 2010. This section shall take effect upon approval of the electors.

Section 29. Limitation on the Assessed Value of Real Property Used for Residential Purposes

(a) The repeal of the renewable energy source property tax exemption in Section 3 of Article VII shall take effect upon approval by the voters.

(b) The amendment to Section 4 of Article VII authorizing the legislature to prohibit an increase in the assessed value of real property used for residential purposes as the result of improving the property's resistance to wind damage or installing a renewable energy source device shall take effect January 1, 2009.

Section 30. Assessment of Working Waterfront Property

The amendment to Section 4 of Article VII providing for the assessment of working waterfront property based on current use, and this section, shall take effect upon approval by the electors and shall first apply to assessments for tax years beginning January 1, 2010.

Section 31. Additional Ad Valorem Tax Exemption for Certain Members of the Armed Forces Deployed on Active Duty Outside of the United States

The amendment to Section 3 of Article VII providing for an additional ad valorem tax exemption for members of the United States military or military reserves, the United States Coast

Guard or its reserves, or the Florida National Guard deployed on active duty outside of the United States in support of military operations designated by the legislature and this section shall take effect January 1, 2011.

Section 32. Veterans Disabled Due to Combat Injury; Homestead Property Tax Discount
The amendment to subsection (e) of Section 6 of Article VII relating to the homestead property tax discount for veterans who became disabled as the result of a combat injury shall take effect January 1, 2013.

Section 33. Ad Valorem Tax Relief for Surviving Spouses of Veterans Who Died From Service-Connected Causes and First Responders Who Died in the Line Of Duty
This section and the amendment to Section 6 of Article VII permitting the legislature to provide ad valorem tax relief to surviving spouses of veterans who died from service-connected causes and first responders who died in the line of duty shall take effect January 1, 2013.

Section 34. Solar Devices or Renewable Energy Source Devices; Exemption From Certain Taxation and Assessment
This section, the amendment to subsection (e) of Section 3 of Article VII authorizing the legislature, subject to limitations set forth in general law, to exempt the assessed value of solar devices or renewable energy source devices subject to tangible personal property tax from ad valorem taxation, and the amendment to subsection (i) of Section 4 of Article VII authorizing the legislature, by general law, to prohibit the consideration of the installation of a solar device or a renewable energy source device in determining the assessed value of real property for the purpose of ad valorem taxation shall take effect on January 1, 2018, and shall expire on December 31, 2037. Upon expiration, this section shall be repealed and the text of subsection (e) of Section 3 of Article VII and subsection (i) of Section 4 of Article VII shall revert to that in existence on

December 31, 2017, except that any amendments to such text otherwise adopted shall be preserved and continue to operate to the extent that such amendments are not dependent upon the portions of text which expire pursuant to this section.

Section 35. Tax Exemption for Totally and Permanently Disabled First Responders
The amendment to Section 6 of Article VII relating to relief from ad valorem taxes assessed on homestead property for first responders, who are totally and permanently disabled as a result of injuries sustained in the line of duty, takes effect January 1, 2017.

Section 36. Additional Ad Valorem Exemption for Persons Age Sixty-Five or Older
This section and the amendment to Section 6 of Article VII revising the just value determination for the additional ad valorem tax exemption for persons age sixty-five or older shall take effect January 1, 2017, following approval by the electors, and shall operate retroactively to January 1, 2013, for any person who received the exemption under paragraph (2) of Section 6(d) of Article VII before January 1, 2017.

www.ingramcontent.com/pod-product-compliance
Lightning Source LLC
Chambersburg PA
CBHW052252220526
45471CB00001B/303